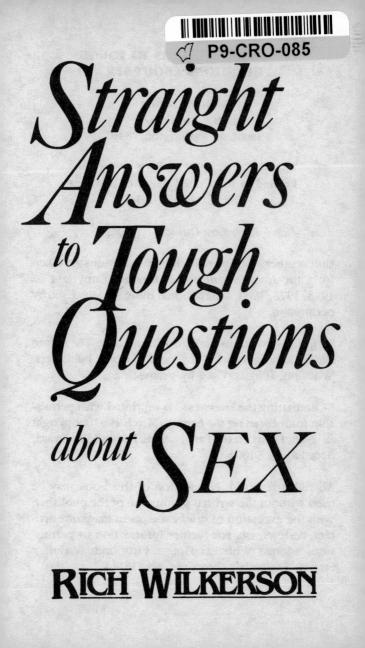

P9-CRO-085

Straight Answers to Tough Questions about SEX

RICH WILKERSON

STRAIGHT ANSWERS TO TOUGH
QUESTIONS ABOUT SEX

Rich Wilkerson
P.O. Box 1092
Tacoma, Washington 98401

Edited by David L. Young

**Dedicated to
My Three Sons:**

Jonfulton Wesley
Richard Preston Jr.
Graham Timothy Buntain

In faith, believing that they
will stand pure for Jesus Christ!

ACKNOWLEDGEMENTS

Thanks to my Lord and Savior Jesus Christ for giving me life more abundantly.

Thanks to my most treasured gift from God outside of salvation, my wife Robyn, whom I love.

Thanks to Peggy Kainz for her help with the typing of this manuscript.

Thanks to David L. Young for editorial assistance.

Thanks to Mr. Bob Whitaker for his love for God and for precious young adults who need this printed help.

CONTENTS

INTRODUCTION

We live in a society that lacks moral decency. Children across this land are forced to grow up much sooner than in any previous generation. Consequently, young people are noted for acting before asking.

This is especially true in terms of human sexuality. What a mess this has produced. Over 1,000,000 teenagers get pregnant each year in the United States. Over 400,000 of those pregnancies are aborted.

Statistics tell us that 70 percent of high school male seniors have had sexual intercourse. Over 50 percent of high school female seniors have had sexual intercourse. One in five girls will have sex before the age of thirteen.

I've mentioned these statistics for a reason: The moral breakdown facing North American single adults is a result of an immoral pattern established much earlier in life.

Teenagers have bigger bodies than brains. As time passes, those brains begin to catch up with their bodies, and the questions begin to fly. Young adults often experience the desire to go back and change yesterday.

Since 1972, I've had the privilege of working with single adults, and I've heard many of their questions during this time. I have written this book to try and answer from the Bible the questions singles most often ask about sex.

The first half of the book will deal with what I believe is God's clear-cut plan for male and female relationships—*The 4 D's of Dating*.

The second half of the book, *Common Questions Concerning Single Adult Sexuality*, will cover specific questions and answers. Each chapter ends with some questions you should consider and some Bible verses that will help you both now and in the future.

My desire is that *Straight Answers To Tough Questions About Sex* will help you develop moral purity as you seek God's will concerning a life-time partner.

PART I:

THE
4 D's
OF DATING

*God's plan for male/female
relationships*

DESIGN

1

DESIGN

Dating can be one of the most exciting experiences of a person's life, or it can be disastrous. Thankfully, God has given scriptural guidelines to make dating a pleasure. I call them *The Four D's of Dating*.

The first "D" is *design*. God has a design for our lives that, for the vast majority of us, culminates in marriage. I suspect that most of you are believing God for a mate. The most important relationship, other than your relationship with Jesus Christ, is the one that will develop between you and that member of the opposite sex who will become your lifelong partner in marriage.

It was God who created the idea of marriage. In Genesis 2:18, the Bible records that God looked down upon Adam and said, "It is not good that the man should be alone." While in the Garden of Eden, Adam had many different animals and birds to watch over and rule, but none of these creatures satisfied his need for companionship.

So God formed a woman from Adam's rib to provide him with the beautiful love relationship we call "marriage."

But prior to marriage we engage in the incredible activity known as *dating*. Some of you may not have dated yet. Others have taken a few steps in this area, and still others have already been hurt in dating relationships.

Dating: Growing Together Spiritually

Dating should bring two people together spiritually. Galatians 5:22-23 lists the nine fruits of the Spirit: "But the fruit of the Spirit is love, joy, peace, longsuffering, gentleness, goodness, faith, meekness, temperance: against such there is no law" (*KJV*). Let's take each one of these different kinds of spiritual fruit and consider them in light of the dating relationship.

1. *Love*

The love mentioned in this passage from Galatians is *agape* love. Agape love implies respect, not physical attraction. Men who stare at a woman as she strolls by and exclaim, "Wow!" are certainly not showing her respect. That is not agape love.

When I speak of *agape* love, I am speaking of one of the four kinds of love the early Greeks defined. The other three Greek loves are *storge, phileo,* and *eros.*.

Storge love is the kind of love a family experiences. It is developed from birth with our family members.

Phileo love is based upon common interests with others. This is the kind of love experienced among good friends.

Eros love is determined by sexual/sensual desire. Eros love is most often based upon feelings.

Phileo and eros are the two loves most everyone can readily relate to. Why? Because these loves are both founded upon "conditions" and "feelings."

These loves say, "You must meet my conditions or make me feel good before we can have any kind of relationship."

Agape love, however, is based upon a person's personal choice and commitment to another person. It says, "All of my choices as they relate to you will always be for your highest good and best interest." Avoid anything in your dating relationships that destroys respect for another person.

2. *Joy*

The second fruit of the Spirit is joy. Our daily relationships should be characterized by the presence of joy. We should enjoy ourselves in a manner that pleases God when we're dating that special person.

Does your dating behavior glorify God? If not, then change it! If there is any doubt about the propriety of your dating activities, may I suggest that you look at them from God's point of view? If you think the Lord is frowning upon an activity you and your date are participating in, then abstain from that activity. You will have no true joy if you are displeasing God.

3. *Peace*

The third fruit of the Spirit is peace. When you're on a date—and I don't care how old you are or how many people you're with—you and your partner need to share a quiet time with the Lord. After all, He made everything you are enjoying together. You should praise God together even if you're out playing tennis or softball. Everything you could possibly experience was created and planned by the Lord. He should be praised!

Prior to our marriage, my wife and I had quiet times on our dates. During these special times, we would share together in reading the Bible and praying. They proved to be some of our warmest times together.

You may be thinking, That sounds corny. But let me remind you, friend, that the possibility of spending the next fifty years of your life with the person you are now dating should drive both of you to your knees in prayer.

If your relationship with each other begins with the common ground of prayer and Bible study, the peace that results will take you through the trying times of marriage in the future.

4. *Longsuffering*

The fourth fruit of the Spirit is longsuffering. We need to be patient and wait for the right person. Some people are so antsy that they will never find the right person. They're not longsuffering. The only thing on their mind is finding somebody as quickly as possible! Often people are not willing to wait for God's timing, and eventually they reap a lifetime of sorrow because of their impatience and impulsiveness.

Many people who come to me for counsel have their entire lives wrapped up in finding a partner. That's all they care about. They don't care about the will of God, and they don't care about their lives. All they are concerned about is, "He didn't notice me tonight"; or "He doesn't care about me"; or "She doesn't even look at me."

The twenty-fourth chapter of Genesis describes one of the most moving love stories in all of Scripture—the story of Isaac and Rebecca and how God used Isaac's father to bring the two together.

Isaac was a young man who rarely, if ever, dated. One day his dad said, "I'm going to find somebody for you, son." What Isaac did *not* do was turn several shades of red and yell, "I'll check the territory myself, Dad! Back off!" Instead, he willingly submitted to his father's wishes. Isaac's father, Abraham, sent his servant to his distant homeland with instructions to find a girl of similar ethnic heritage.

Many young people rebel against everything their folks have told them regarding dating and developing relationships. They think their parents are totally incapable of knowing their needs for a lifetime partner. That's not the case at all. Believe it or not, God has given parents some great insights. This proved true in Isaac's case.

Actually, "dating" is not a biblical concept but rather a product of our Western culture. In Old and New Testament times, parents chose their children's lifetime partner. Parents should still be involved in their children's decisions about a marriage partner. Kids who rebel against their parents are headed for trouble.

I wonder what thoughts paraded through Isaac's mind. You can imagine him thinking, "I'll bet he's going to bring home some kind of beast." I'm sure Isaac was busy interceding before God. This whole situation probably drove him daily to his knees, crying, "Almighty God, speak to my dad's servant. Direct his eyes. Direct his whole body. Lord, don't let him come home with some . . . oh, God, please!"

Meanwhile, Abraham's servant was in constant prayer, asking God to direct him. And every prayer he prayed was answered. His attention was soon drawn to a beautiful young lady named Rebecca, who was drawing water from a well. He went to her parents' home and asked their consent to take her back to Isaac. Rebecca received permission and accompanied the servant back to Abraham's home.

As she and the servant drew near, Isaac happened to be out in the field praying. Suddenly he looked up and saw camels approaching in the distance. He had been longsuffering for many years, and finally he saw the servant coming with a beautiful young lady.

She asked, "Who's that?"

The servant replied, "That's my master." Then she covered her face, for that was the custom in those days. Isaac gazed at her and she at him. I'm sure they both exchanged "Hallelujahs." Then they were married—all because a wise father had given godly counsel and instruction to his servant about what his son needed. Remember, too, that Issac had been longsuffering and didn't disregard his father's wishes. God brought together a beautiful union.

My heartfelt encouragement to young people is this: Don't run away from your parents' advice. It's important! Your folks have made mistakes that they can help you avoid. Don't rebel against them. *Listen to them*. They will help you in this area of longsuffering and patience.

5. *Gentleness*

A fifth fruit of the Spirit is gentleness. Don't demand attention on your dates. You are there to have a good time. Some men think they must be the life of the party in order to impress their dating partner, but a woman is often more embarrassed than proud of an attention-seeking escort.

Be gentle and considerate at all times—not rude or loudmouthed. Consider your date's needs as more important than your own.

6. *Goodness*

The seventh fruit, goodness, tells us to be kind to one another. The good that you show a person will long be remembered. I thank God for the continued friendship of people whom I dated prior to marriage. I didn't rip them off, and they didn't rip me off. We were good to one another and were able to be proud of our goodness. Let goodness reign in your relationships.

7. *Faith*

Next is the fruit of faith. Make every one of your dates a faith date. What am I saying? Just this: DO NOT DATE UNBELIEVERS! Here is what *The Living Bible* says in 2 Corinthians 6:14:

> Don't be teamed with those who do not love the Lord, for what do the people of God have in common with the people of sin? How can light live with darkness?

In short, how can a Christian live with a sinner?

Many ladies say, "Well, I'm just going out with him because I've asked God to give me a mission field. I want to bring him to Jesus." If you really care that much about him, ask one of the men in your fellowship to bring him to church.

Ladies, don't worry about taking him to church because he's probably got other ideas. The same goes for men. Forget about "missionary dating." Send another lady to lead her to Jesus. Remember, every marriage starts with a date.

When it comes to this matter of personal dating, the Bible warns us to separate ourselves from ungodliness and from non-Christians.

> And what harmony can there be between Christ and the devil? How can a Christian be a partner with one who doesn't believe? And what union can there be between God's temple and idols? For you are God's temple, the home of the living God, and God has said of you, "I will live in them and walk among them, and I will be their God and they shall be my people." That is why the Lord has said, "Leave them; separate yourselves from them; don't touch their filthy things, and I will welcome you, and be a Father to you, and you will be my sons and daughters"—2 Corinthians 6:15-17, *TLB*.

I'm stunned by the number of young ladies who have come to me with tears streaming down their cheeks, saying, "Rich, when I looked at him I liked him; when I liked him I loved him; when I loved him I let him; and when I let him I lost him." I have heard this time and time again.

Strive to make every date a faith date! If someone you're interested in is not a born-again Christian—and, even beyond that, if they don't share your same persuasion theologically—stay away. I've seen too much quarreling and too many problems in marriages between people of different faiths or denominations. If you'll only be patient, God will bring to you that special person right out of your own circle of friends.

8. *Meekness*

Do you know what meekness is? Meekness is balance. You need to have balance in your dating. Let me tell you what an unhealthy date is—three hours of kissing and five minutes of miniature golf. That's what we call an "unbalanced date."

The Bible says, "The Lord abhors dishonest scales, but accurate weights are his delight" (Proverbs 11:1).

9. *Temperance*

Finally, the last fruit is temperance. This is self-control. In your dating relationships, make sure you exercise self-control. Don't do anything that would harm the other person emotionally. Ladies, you can help the men in this area. Whenever a guy tries to go too far, raise your hand and crack him right in the mouth. Ecclesiastes 9:10 says, "Whatever thy hand findeth to do, do it with all thy might." In the name of the Lord, whack! I say this with "tongue in cheek," but I do want to stress the importance of self-control.

Always conduct yourself on your date as though Christ were present. *He is!* I hear young men say all the time, "I can't help what I do when I'm with her because I'm in love." My friend David Roever says, "That young man isn't in love—he's in heat."

Listen to me, men and women: You are not a slave to your glands. You *can* control yourself with God's help. Remember, it is impossible for real love to exist without respect. You must have self-control.

Engagement: Get To Know Each Other

We've seen that the first part of God's design in male and female relationships is dating. The second part of God's design is engagement. The purpose of this period in a relationship is to bring two people together emotionally and allow them time to discover how the other views life. When faced with a problem, how does she respond? How does he react?

I knew a woman who was engaged to someone who literally blew up at the drop of a hat. She would laugh it off and excuse him, "Isn't that sweet what he just did? He's demonstrative, you know. He gets real upset because he loves me so much."

Infatuation had blinded them. They didn't realize that they had a serious problem, so they got married. Six months later she cried herself to sleep at night: "Dear God in heaven, is he going to keep this up?" The engagement period is vital in helping people discover more about one another.

Marriage: A Total Union

Finally, we come to the area in God's design called marriage. His plan is to mold together two people's hearts, minds, and bodies in perfect harmony. The physical act of intercourse in marriage is the most intimate of all physical relationships. I want to touch on four reasons why God has given us sexual activity in marriage.

1. *Friendship*

First, God gave us sex in marriage for friendship. When we speak of sex, we are not only speaking of the physical act of love but also the bond that forms between a man and a woman. That bond grows into a beautiful friendship.

2. *Pleasure*

The second reason for a sexual relationship in marriage is that of pleasure. This is the main reason for the sexual habits of non-Christians. They think the *only* purpose of sex is pleasure.

These people can be called "pleasure mongers" because that's all they're interested in. They "use" other people. Their whole life is built on feelings, and they laugh at the old-fashioned values—'I don't care what the cost is; I want to feel good!" The Bible says, "Sin has its pleasure for a season" . . . but then comes payday! In reality, "pleasure mongers" are some of the most miserable people on earth.

God did give us sex for pleasure, but only within the boundaries of marriage. We are not to think that intercourse is bad. It's beautiful—in marriage. Prior to marriage, we are not emotionally capable of handling sexual intercourse.

If we've taken this beautiful act of love and hauled it through the mud with different partners, then we're going into the marriage bed plagued with all kinds of nagging thoughts: "I wonder who else he (or she) did this with. I wonder if they love me as much as all those other people they've. . . ."

All these thoughts prey on our minds, and soon the sexual part of the marriage is ruined. God created sex for pleasure, yes, but we are only to experience it within the confines of marriage. This rule is for our protection!

I want to emphasize that *God* created sex, not the devil. The devil has tried to get attention and recognition by making God's creation filthy. He often takes the good things of God and twists and perverts them.

As Christians, the devil would love to make us think we have an option. Let me remind you that there is no recourse other than the Word of God for a born-again believer. And with God's strength, you can abide by His Word.

3. *Reproduction*

The third reason for sex is reproduction. Many early Christians thought reproduction was the only reason for sex. They thought, "It's terribly filthy. Don't ever mention it or bring it up. We have to do this in order to have more children so they can carry on this terrible tradition."

In reality, we have the awesome privilege to be co-creators with the Lord. Every baby manifests God's belief in the future.

4. *Protection*

The fourth reason is for protection, both physically and spiritually. Syphilis, gonorrhea, and various other types of venereal diseases—herpes simplex II, AIDS, etc.—have spread across this nation and literally around the world because of immorality. These social diseases, which come as a result of immorality, have a spiritual root. God gave us sex in marriage for physical protection. He protects those who live pure for Him.

In addition, God has given us this act of love in marriage to protect us spiritually. Everyone has been tempted and tried in this area of sexual desire. The devil throws this into our faces and accuses and condemns us for our sexual failures. But when we stay within God's limits, we give the devil no opportunity to trap us.

These are four parts of God's plan that are reserved for marriage in the area of sex. Since intercourse is the most intimate and precious of all physical relationships God has given us, I want you to have a new respect for God's love and for the sexual aspect of your relationship in marriage.

The way you can get the maximized best from this gift of love from God is by sharing it with someone like-minded in spiritual matters. That is God's ultimate design in dating and marriage.

Let's Review

Do you remember?

1. God's purpose in dating is to bring two people together in what way?
2. Which of the fruits of the Spirit talks about waiting for that *right* person?
3. Whom does God most often use to give you direction and wisdom in your dating life?
4. What is the main "taboo" in dating?
5. In the engagement period, how does God bring two people together?
6. How does God mold two people together through marriage?
7. Can you name two reasons why God gives us a sexual relationship in marriage?

Ask yourself:

1. Have I violated God's design in my dating relationships?
2. Is it easy to slip into a panic, thinking that God has forgotten me and won't give me the right date or marriage partner?
3. Is God in control of my dating life? If not, how would it change things if He were?
4. Do my date and I help each other grow as Christians?
5. What are my reasons (motives) for wanting to date? (Be honest with yourself!)

6. What things do I have in common with unbelievers? What things do I not have in common?

Try this:

Talk to your pastor or your parents and ask them this question: "What is the most important thing you could share with me about dating?" (They will be pleasantly surprised that you thought them wise enough to ask!) Listen carefully to what they say. Hopefully, a good, open conversation will develop.

Study these scriptures:

"He carries out his decree against me and many such plans he still has in store"— Job 23:14.

"For the Lord God is a sun and shield; the Lord bestows favor and honor; no good thing does he withhold from those whose walk is blameless"— Psalm 84:11.

"Charm is deceptive, and beauty is fleeting; but a woman who fears the Lord is to be praised"— Proverbs 31:30.

"Like a gold ring in a pig's snout is a beautiful woman who shows no discretion"—Proverbs 11:22.

"But seek first his kingdom and his righteousness, and all these things will be given to you as well"— Matthew 6:33.

"Love the Lord your God with all your heart and with all your soul and with all your mind and with all your strength. The second is this: 'Love your neighbor as yourself.' There is no commandment greater than these'—Mark 12:30-31.

"I would like you to be free from concern. An unmarried man is concerned about the Lord's affairs—how he can please the Lord. But a married man is concerned about the affairs of this world—how he can please his wife—and his interests are divided. An unmarried woman or virgin is concerned about the Lord's affairs: Her aim is to be devoted to the Lord in both body and spirit. But a married woman is concerned about the affairs of this world—how she can please her husband. I am saying this for your own good, not to restrict you but that you may live in a right way in undivided devotion to the Lord"—1 Corinthians 7:32-35.

"Do not be misled: "Bad company corrupts good character"—1 Corinthians 15:33.

DESIRE

2

DESIRE

The second "D" for Christian dating is *desire*. All of us have experienced a desire for the opposite sex. It's a God-given desire. In Genesis 2:35, God said, "For this reason will a man leave his father and mother and be united to his wife, and they will become one flesh." This God-given desire for the opposite sex is intended to be culminated in marriage.

I cannot stress enough how important it is to guard your desires and keep them under control. "It is better to marry than to burn with passion," said the apostle Paul (1 Corinthians 7:9). What does that mean? He was saying that it is better to marry than to be consumed by desire.

A tragic story in the Old Testament in 2 Samuel 13 tells about a young man who didn't control his passion. His name was Prince Amnon, and he was a son of King David. He fell desperately in love with his half-sister, Tamar, but failed to guard his God-given desires. Amnon was literally tormented by his love for her, but, since the girls and young men were kept strictly apart, he had no way of talking to her.

Amnon finally found a solution. Deciding to act like he was sick, he persuaded a friend to bring Tamar into his bedroom to prepare him something to eat. The friend approached Tamar and said, "Listen, your brother Amnon is sick, and he wants you to bring him some food to help him get better."

She went into Amnon's bedroom so he could watch her mix some dough. Then she baked some special bread for him. But when she set the serving tray before him, he refused to eat it. Instead, he ordered everyone out of the room. Then, turning to Tamar, Amnon said, "Bring me the food again here in my bedroom and feed it to me." As she was standing before him, he grabbed her and demanded, "Come lie with me, my sister."

Tamar was horrified. She was a godly young lady and wanted to do what was right. "Oh Amnon!" she cried. "Don't be foolish. Don't do this to me. You know what a serious crime it is in Israel. Where could I go in my shame? You'd be called one of the greatest fools in Israel. Please, just speak to the king about it, for he will let you marry me." But he wouldn't listen to her, and since he was stronger than she, he forced her.

In other words, he *raped* her. He didn't guard his desires. But no sooner had he raped her than

34

his love for her turned to hate; the Bible says he hated her even more than he had loved her. "Get out of here," he snarled.

The apostle Paul wrote in 1 Corinthians 9:27, in effect, "I keep my body under control"—that is, he kept his affections, his body, and everything about himself under the Holy Spirit's control. Amnon had been raised in a godly home, but he refused to guard his desires. Eventually, the desire for lust destroyed him. Several years later, Absalom, his half-brother and the brother of Tamar, killed Amnon because of the shameful act he had committed against his sister. Amnon's lust cost him his life.

The Works of the Flesh

1. *Adultery*

When the desire for the opposite sex gets out of control, it is easy to yield to the works of the flesh. These works are described in Galatians 5:19-21:

> Now the works of the flesh are manifest, which are these; Adultery, fornication, uncleanness, lasciviousness, idolatry, witchcraft, hatred, variance, emulations, wrath, strife, seditions, heresies, envyings, murders, drunkenness, revellings, and such like—*KJV*.

Adultery is sexual intercourse with someone other than your husband or wife. Exodus 20:14 forbids this: "Thou shalt not commit adultery." James 2:11 also talks about it.

2. *Fornication*

The second work of the flesh listed in Galatians 5 is fornication, which is engaging in sexual intercourse before marriage. Acts 15:21, 2 Corinthians 6:13, and 1 Thessalonians 4:3 all talk about fornication. In fact, the Bible says in Revelation 21:8 that all fornicators will go to hell if they don't repent and get right with God.

3. *Uncleanness*

The third work of the flesh is uncleanness. This is living in immorality outside of the Spirit of God. Uncleanness leads us into the next three important areas:

4. *Lasciviousness*

Lasciviousness is mentioned in Galatians 5:19 and has to do with stirring up sensual thoughts—reading dirty magazines or pornography, going to dirty movies, and generally involving yourself with things that arouse the sensual chord in your life. Other scriptures that deal with lasciviousness are Mark 7:22 and Ephesians 4:19.

Jude 4 says,

> For there are certain men crept in unawares, who were before of old ordained to this condemnation, ungodly men, turning the grace of our God into lasciviousness, and denying the only Lord God, and our Lord Jesus Christ—*KJV*.

Here lasciviousness is compared to denying the Christian faith.

5. *Concupiscence*

Two other works of the flesh not listed in Galatians 5:19 go beyond lasciviousness. The first is concupiscence, mentioned in Romans 7:8, Colossians 3:5, and 1 Thessalonians 4:5. While lasciviousness means stirring up sensual thoughts, concupiscence is *dwelling* on them.

Many people are in bondage to filthy movies, pornography, and trashy books. Satan always tries to short-circuit our God-given desires with a quick-fix approach to sexual happiness. It never works.

Not long ago a fine looking eighteen year-old came to one of my meetings. Dressed in a three-piece suit, he played in the church orchestra and praised God all through the service. But after everyone had gone, he asked if we could talk for a few minutes.

He confessed, "For about three years now, I just haven't been able to get pornography out of my life. I've got dirty books under my mattress and all kinds of pictures posted in my locker at school and at the gym. They're in my room everywhere—but out of my parents' sight. It's all I ever think about. How can I be delivered?" Caught in the trap of concupiscence, this young man had been allowing sex to control his thought-life.

I told him, "To begin with, destroy all of the material. After all, how can you walk into a room filled with pictures of naked people and shout, 'Hallelujah! It doesn't affect me'? Remove the filthy things from before your eyes and ask God to deliver you." By the end of the meeting, God had delivered him. Caught in the trap of concupiscence, he had been allowing sex to control his thought-life.

6. *Reprobation*

Those who go beyond concupiscence step into the last of the works of the flesh—reprobation—which refers to a totally burned-out conscience. Reprobate individuals have dwelt on immorality and sensual material for so long that they have lost their conscience and no longer feel it is wrong to be involved in these things. Whether you're saved or unsaved, the first time you looked at something that you shouldn't have been looking at, you were stricken with an intense feeling of guilt—"Wow, I shouldn't have done that." That was your conscience.

When someone dwells on sensual activity continuously for a long period of time, he comes to a place where his mind is unable to discern the difference between right and wrong. The conscience is seared. He has burned himself out. And often that's the point at which the person's craving for sensual things becomes an obsession. He searches for new and radical ways to satisfy his sexual desires. When this happens, the door to homosexual or lesbian relationships is opened.

The first chapter of Romans describes people who involve themselves in filth so much that they begin to look upon members of the same sex with lust. That's what is happening in our country today. We've come to such a place of reprobation that one in ten Americans is now adamantly happy to profess his homosexuality. It's incredible!

It has often been said that good things come to those who wait. The Bible tells us that Jacob worked a total of fourteen years to receive the hand of Rachel in marriage. Because Jacob bridled his God-given "desire," God was able to trust him in a unique way. From Jacob's life came the twelve patriarchs of Israel.

I have never counseled a couple planning to marry who were not struggling to control their sexual desire. It is natural! It is God-given! It is good! I can say from firsthand experience, however, that those who wait will experience a great life together and, more importantly, a growing desire for each other.

Remember, our body is the temple of the Holy Spirit—God's house. Let's keep it holy.

Let's Review

Do you remember?

1. Who gave us the desire for the opposite sex?
2. 1 Corinthians 7:9 says: "It is better to marry than to burn _____ ."
3. What was the name of the young man who raped his half-sister, and what happened to him as a result of his sin?
4. What is the work of the flesh that means to dwell on sensual thoughts?
5. What is the term that describes a burned-out conscience?

Ask yourself:

1. Am I controlling my "desire," or is my "desire" controlling me?
2. What are some ways that, with God's help, I can keep from doing with my desires what Amnon did with his?
3. Is the strongest desire in my life to have a deep and meaningful relationship with the Lord Jesus Christ, or do I have other desires that are taking the place of this most important goal?

Try this!

Go to your pastor, parents, or somebody you feel comfortable talking with and share your struggles with your "desires." Have them pray with you. They will understand. Be sure to talk to your heavenly Father about these things, too.

Destroy all the things you possess that keep your "desires" out of control. (Don't forget about the young man who had trouble with pornography.)

Study these scriptures:

"I made a covenant with my eyes not to look lustfully at a girl"—Job 31:1.

"Treat younger men as brothers, older women as mothers, and younger women as sisters, with absolute purity"—1 Timothy 5:2.

"Your beauty should not come from outward adornment, such as braided hair and the wearing of gold jewelry and fine clothes. Instead, it should be that of your inner self, the unfading beauty of a gentle and quiet spirit, which is of great worth in God's sight"—1 Peter 3:3-4.

"Do you not know that your body is a temple of the Holy Spirit, who is in you, whom you have received from God? You are not your own"—1 Corinthians 6:19.

"Don't you know that you yourselves are God's temple and that God's Spirit lives in you?"—1 Corinthians 3:16.

"Do not be overcome by evil, but overcome evil with good"—Romans 12:21.

"Rather clothe yourselves with the Lord Jesus Christ, and do not think about how to gratify the desires of the sinful nature"—Romans 13:14.

"Set your minds on things above, not on earthly things"—Colossians 3:2.

"You have heard that it was said, 'Do not commit adultery.' But I tell you that anyone who looks at a woman lustfully has already committed adultery with her in his heart"—Matthew 5:27-28.

"For of this you can be sure: No immoral, impure or greedy person—such a man is an idolater—has any inheritance in the kingdom of Christ and of God"—Ephesians 5:5.

DECLINE

3

DECLINE

The third "D" after design and desire is *decline*. God is calling Christian people to decline immorality—to say "no" to it. God wants us to decline filthiness, walk in His love, and move in His design (as opposed to the devil's).

Solomon said in Proverbs 1:10, "My son [daughter], if sinners entice you ['Come on. Let's go get drunk. Let's go smoke some dope. Let's go get it on by the lake after we go to Sunday night church.'], do not give in to them."

If sinners entice you, decline the enticement! Decline the invitation: "Sorry, I'm saved. I love God!"

Maybe you're wondering, Why should we decline? Solomon tells us in Proverbs 7:6-23,

> I was looking out the window of my house one day, and saw a simple-minded lad, walking in twilight down the street to the house of this wayward girl, a

prostitute. She approached him, saucy and pert, and dressed seductively. She was the brash, coarse type, seen often in the streets and markets, soliciting at every corner for men to be her lovers.

She put her arms around him and kissed him, and with a saucy look she said, "I have decided to forget our quarrel! I was just coming to look for you and here you are! My bed is spread with lovely, colored sheets of the finest linen, imported from Egypt, perfumed with myrrh, aloes and cinnamon. Come on, let's take our fill of love until morning, for my husband is away on a long trip. He has taken a wallet full of money with him, and won't return for several days."

So she seduced him with her pretty speech, her coaxing and her wheedling, until he yielded to her. He couldn't resist her flattery. He followed her as an ox going to the butcher, or as a stag that is trapped, waiting to be killed with an arrow through the heart. He was as a bird flying into a snare, not knowing the fate awaiting it there.

Listen to me, young men [and you young ladies, as well], and not only listen but obey; don't let your desires get out of hand; don't let yourself think about her [or him]. Don't go near her [or him]; stay away from where she [or he] walks, lest she [or he] tempt you and seduce you. For she [or he] has been the ruin of multitudes—a vast host of men [or women] have been her [or his] victims. If you want to find the road to hell, look for her [or his] house—*TLB*.

You ask, "Why should we decline the invitation?" Think about it: Do you want to go to hell? Not really? Then be well-advised by Proverbs 7.

Genesis chapter thirty-nine tells a story about a godly young man named Joseph who declined the invitation to sin. Joseph was put in total charge of his master's house. One day while his master, Potiphar, was away on a trip, Potiphar's wife approached Joseph to seduce him. She urged repeatedly, "Come on. Come to bed with me." Joseph was a pure young man who wasn't about to lose his virginity. He exclaimed, "How . . . can I do this great wickedness, and sin against God?" (Genesis 39:9, *KJV*).

My earnest appeal to all people is to decline the devil's invitation to come together sexually. Learn to say "No." Decide that before you are confronted with the actual situation and temptation. If you don't decline the invitation, you will bring upon yourself great wickedness, and you'll break the heart of God. He's a loving Father.

There is nothing more lovely and precious than a bride who has preserved her virtue for her husband. She walks down the aisle in a beautiful white dress, a symbol of her purity.

Likewise, nothing is quite as strong or *powerful* as a man on his wedding day receiving his bride with his virtue and virginity intact. He's clean and pure before God.

When a person is willing to decline Satan's invitation to sin morally, he or she is taking a strong stand for God and His Word. For this is God's "design."

I personally believe that intense spiritual attack often comes right before a great spiritual victory. If you have been under continual barrage from Satan's arsenal of fiery sexual darts, most likely you are on the verge of a tremendous victory. Hold on to God's Word.

Let's Review

Do you remember?

1. What is God calling all Christian people, including you, to decline?
2. What happened to the young man in Proverbs chapter 7 who met the prostitute on the street corner?

Ask yourself:

1. What benefits will I receive if I decline immorality and live God's way?
2. Is it hard for me to say "No?" If so, why?
3. Is God controlling my thought life?
4. Do my date and I talk much about the things of God? (Christ should be the central focus of your relationship.)

Try this!

Make a list of all the reasons you have decided to decline immorality. Then call your dating partner and have an honest discussion about the purity necessary for you to retain in your dating life. Talk openly about your standards. Pray together. Be sure to read the list together periodically.

Study these scriptures:

"But Daniel resolved not to defile himself with the royal food and wine, and he asked the chief official for permission not to defile himself this way"—Daniel 1:8.

"No temptation has seized you except what is common to man. And God is faithful; he will not let you be tempted beyond what you can bear. But when you are tempted, he will also provide a way out so that you can stand up under it"—1 Corinthians 10:13.

"And let us consider how we may spur one another on toward love and good deeds"—Hebrews 10:24.

"Finally, brothers, whatever is true, whatever is noble, whatever is right, whatever is pure, whatever is lovely, whatever is admirable—if anything is excellent or praiseworthy—think about such things"—Philippians 4:8.

"Do you not know that your bodies are members of Christ himself? Shall I then take the members of Christ and unite them with a prostitute? Never! Do you not know that he who unites himself with a prostitute is one with her in body? For it is said, 'The two will become one flesh.' But he who unites himself with the Lord is one with him in spirit. Flee from sexual immorality. All other sins a man commits are outside his body, but he who sins sexually sins against his own body. Do you not know that your body is a temple of the Holy Spirit, who is in you, whom you have received from God? You are not your own, you were bought at a price. Therefore honor God with your body''—1 Corinthians 6:15-20.

''When tempted, no one should say, 'God is tempting me.' For God cannot be tempted by evil, nor does he tempt anyone; but each one is tempted when, by his own evil desire, he is dragged away and enticed. Then, after desire has conceived, it gives birth to sin; and sin, when it is full-grown, gives birth to death''—James 1:13-15.

DELIGHT

4

DELIGHT

The fourth and final "D" is *delight*. The years of your youth are the years of delight. They should not be spoiled by a failure to live God's way.

A young woman wept before me not long ago, "Mr. Wilkerson, my boyfriend just broke my heart." I told her, "You had no business giving your heart away!" Young ladies have no business giving their hearts away to just any guy. The same holds true for guys.

I'd like to stress an important point for the sake of the young ladies. Don't fling yourself at guys. Be a challenge. You'd be surprised how guys will respond to a challenge! If a guy picks you up for a date and doesn't open the door, let him drive away by himself.

One reason for a lack of delight in relationships these days is that young adults are in too much of a hurry to develop a heavy relationship with one another. They're not patient. I don't think young people should date by themselves until they're at least sixteen years old. Obviously, they'll be relating to the opposite sex in group activities long before that time. But it is best to wait until their brain catches up with their body before they start dating.

Let me ask a question: If a teenager is holding hands at twelve and kissing his girlfriend at thirteen, is kissing his girlfriend still going to be fun when he's fifteen? Continual growth is a part of human nature. If they've already experienced the basic levels of male/female affection at thirteen, they will not be satisfied with that when they're fifteen. There's nowhere to go except "all the way." *One of the reasons for a lack of delight is that young people have run way ahead of God's plan for their lives.*

Young adults must wait in silent anticipation. When you hear the word "anticipation," you think of good things. Anticipating means to delay in silent expectation. If we will move in God's planning and timing and avoid getting the cart before the horse, we will experience a great deal of delight.

Once the dating process has begun, ladies should be a challenge. And men need to try harder. Too many men give up and quit if the ladies provide a challenge. I don't mean that men should try harder sexually—I'm talking about being strong and realizing that if a woman challenges you, don't just give up and go over in the corner and sulk. She's worth the challenge. Be strong!

Delighting In God

Psalm 37:4 instructs us, "Delight yourself also in the Lord and he will give you the desires of your heart." I'd like to share how this has worked for me. When I gave my heart to the Lord and started delighting in God, a fantastic change took place in my life. I started looking on young ladies with the right motivation. Before I got my heart right with God, I looked at women with impure motives. Now when I see a beautiful lady, I praise God and thank Him for His lovely handiwork. Ladies can do the same thing when they look at a man. Give God the praise. He made him or her.

The first time I saw my wife-to-be, I was sitting in the church choir. When this gorgeous young lady walked in and sat in the balcony, I gasped, "Oh, hallelujah! Thank you, Lord, for your wonderful handiwork!" I couldn't believe my eyes. I didn't have a chance to meet her that morning, but my father met her in the prayer room after the service that night. She was visiting my city while on vacation from college in Springfield, Missouri.

To my father's surprise, he discovered that he knew her dad. He sensed, "This is the one for my son." My dad had been totally disinterested in every other girl I had dated, but this time it was different. He recognized that she was special. So he came looking for me. "Rich, this is Robyn. Robyn, this is my son." So you see, my father helped me find my wife.

When I saw her, I loved her. Sensing that she was the will of God for my life, I connived a way to see her the next day. Robyn wasn't in a hurry to give her heart away to anybody, so she wasn't overly thrilled to meet me. But I didn't give up. The next day, we got together and talked for three hours as I took her around to see the city.

I asked her to go to a Bible study with me that night, and she said she'd come. It was snowing hard, however, and we got lost. I wound up taking her to some beautiful waterfalls in Minneapolis. She thought, "He's going to try and make out with me." But I didn't—we just walked around and looked at the falls.

The next day I called her, and she couldn't remember me! "Rich, who? Oh, the guy who got lost on the way to the Bible study." Finally I devised a way to get a third date. I figured that she liked me at least a little, and I wanted to impress her before she went back to college.

She drove back to Springfield on a Monday, and that night I called her long distance. Although she was with her boyfriend in the lobby of the school, I said to the person who answered the phone, "I'll wait. Don't hang up." I thought, This woman is a challenge, and I'm not giving up. Her girlfriend yelled down, "There's a Rich Wilkerson from Minneapolis waiting on the phone to speak to you. He says he will wait twenty, thirty, forty minutes—he's waiting until you're done saying goodnight to that guy."

I called her every night until I married her. If I didn't call her, she called me. She gave me her heart. I told the Lord I'd never go out with another girl. Four months after that I told her I loved her, and she told me she loved me. Two months later, I asked her to marry me. She accepted, and seven months later we were married.

We delight in each other. I delight in her, and she delights in me. This happened because we followed God's design. We controlled our desires and declined Satan's invitations to sin.

That all happened in 1972. God has given us beautiful children since that time. Our family is happy because God is in control. That doesn't mean we never argue, but God is our refuge. What He's done for us He can do for every single adult on this planet.

Proverbs 10:24 says, "What the wicked dreads will overtake him; what the righteous desire will be granted." Furthermore, the Word of God declares in Psalm 145:19, "He fulfills the desires of those who fear him; he hears their cry and saves them." God promises to fulfill the desires of the righteous.

What is the desire of a single adult looking for a spouse? The main desire that individual has is to find the right mate. I've talked to many singles who have given up on that desire.

They say, "At this point in my life I'll take anybody who will have me." What a waste. God didn't create any person on this planet to be left out. If your desire is for a spouse and you love the Lord, then I promise you that God had someone in mind just for you before the foundation of the world.

Please don't run ahead of the Lord, and don't fall back and give up, either. Remember, the Word says that if you will seek, you will find.

Let's Review

Do you remember?

1. What is the one thing a young lady needs to be in her relationships with young men?
2. What is one of the key reasons for a lack of delight in a dating relationship?

Ask yourself:

1. How can I bring the "delight" back into my dating life?
2. Am I getting ahead of God? Is my impatience causing me to exhaust all the basic levels of male/female affection? Am I standing on dangerous ground?

Try this!

On all your dates for the next two months, have no physical contact with your date! Let your relationship consist only of meaningful rap sessions, thoughtful words and deeds done toward the other, a challenging project that you both work on, time spent together with your families, Bible study, prayer, etc. You can do it! If not, something is wrong!

Study these scriptures:

"A wife of noble character is her husband's crown, but a disgraceful wife is like decay in his bones"—Proverbs 12:4.

"As iron sharpens iron, so one man sharpens another"—Proverbs 27:17.

"Charm is deceptive, and beauty is fleeting; but a woman who fears the Lord is to be praised"—Proverbs 31:30.

"Be devoted to one another in brotherly love. Honor one another above yourselves"—Romans 12:10.

"Love does no harm to its neighbor. Therefore love is the fulfillment of the law"—Romans 13:10.

"Let us therefore make every effort to do what leads to peace and to mutual edification"—Romans 14:19.

"So whether you eat or drink or whatever you do, do it all for the glory of God"—1 Corinthians 10:31.

"Dear friends, let us love one another, for love comes from God. Everyone who loves has been born of God and knows God. Whoever does not love does not know God, because God is love''—1 John 4:7-8.

''There is no fear in love. But perfect love drives out fear, because fear has to do with punishment. The man who fears is not made perfect in love''—1 John 4:18.

See also 1 Corinthians chapter 13.

CONCLUSION TO PART I

Friend, please listen to me. What I've said in this first part is based on personal experience—from God's Word and from hundreds of counseling sessions with single adults.

Believe me, God really does have a design for your life as it relates to a marriage partner. But remember, it begins with His design in your dating relationships. If you'll follow His design, control your desire, and decline Satan's invitation for immorality, then God will help you to delight in His design.

God loves you, my friend. That's why He has provided these guidelines to proper premarital relationships. *The Four D's of Dating* should serve as a foundation for all of your courting prior to marriage.

With all of the media hype pushing sex today, however, many problems have arisen. We now have Christian discos, Christian night clubs, Christian health clubs, Christian aerobics—all subtle ways of getting singles together. Some Christian singles ministries have become hotbeds for finding new sexual partners!

Recently, a single woman explained that she had accepted Christ several months earlier through a Christian singles program. Several weeks later the man who was in charge of this great outreach ministry asked her for a date. At the close of the dinner date, he said, "Well, since this is our first night out, do you want me to spring for a real nice hotel room, or would you rather just spend the night at my place?"

She just about fainted. She asked, "What does it mean to be a Christian if that's how the leaders act?"

She is not the only person asking questions. Over the last several years, I have received countless letters from singles asking about everything from sexual fantasy to abortion. Because of past sin and failure in this area of morality prior to conversion, many people doubt they can ever change. Others were victims of childhood abuse and molestation. Naturally, today they struggle with other kinds of questions many never face.

In the second half of this book, I will attempt to answer some of these single adults. Obviously, I will not be able to cover all questions, and the questions I will address cannot be covered in their entirety. But I do believe that the answers can literally set people free in Christ Jesus.

Before you proceed, I want you to stop for a moment and ask God to open your heart to understand His biblical position and desire for your life. Possibly some old wounds will resurface. When and if they do, let Jesus heal them once and for all. Remember, the Bible says, "Therefore, if anyone is in Christ, he is a new creation; the old has gone, the new has come!" (2 Corinthians 5:17).

PART II:

COMMON QUESTIONS CONCERNING SINGLE ADULT SEXUALITY

FRIENDSHIP
AND
DATING

5

WHAT ABOUT FRIENDSHIP AND DATING?

Dear Rich,

I've been a Christian for about a year, and I have a question I would like to ask you.

Before I became a Christian, I had sex with several of my boyfriends, but I want to stop now that I am a Christian. This may sound like a dumb question, but just what is the purpose of dating supposed to be for a Christian? And when is friendship a better option than dating?

Before I knew Jesus, I dated to be rowdy, go to parties, and have sex. None of those things are good things to do, and I want to get started on the right foot now that I will be dating as a Christian. Maybe my question seems too simple, but can you help me?

Suzanne

Dear Suzanne,

You have asked the question at the right time! Not only is your question *not* dumb, but you have hit on a real key for your life. Our heavenly Father is pleased with a daughter who is as concerned and eager to do His will as you are. Let me share with you my thinking on the subject of friendship and dating.

You are right in saying that the Lord does not want you dating simply as an excuse to party and have sex. He has a much higher calling on your life than that. As you seek to change your lifestyle, He will be right beside you. God will lead and guide you into the right choices so you can walk closely with Him.

The Lord created within each one of us the desire and need for close, intimate friendships. He placed us within the Body of Christ—the Church—to show us our need to relate to one another.

Satan has taken that desire and warped it. He has convinced this generation through the "sexual revolution" that the way to fulfill the need for intimacy is through sex, and the young adults of this generation have bought the lie wholeheartedly. The results have been devastating.

I'm sure you have seen through your own dating experiences, as well as those of your friends, the pain, sorrow, and feeling of being used that come as a result of sexual relationships outside of the commitment and sharing of marriage. You probably have heard these all too familiar words: "But he said he really loved me and that we were going to get married. Now all I have left are feelings of guilt and shame."

The Lord wants us to see the value of friendships as well as those special relationships that move into dating. He understands your feelings of loneliness and isolation. Being willing to acknowledge these deep feelings is a positive step toward emotional maturity and honesty with God.

The only true source of loving and being loved is found in Christ's agape love, which is love that goes beyond our own feelings and offers unconditional love, forgiveness, and acceptance. It does not say, "I love you *because* . . . " or "I love you *if*. . . . " Agape love says, *"I love you—period."*

Who doesn't want to be loved that way? This is a love that is giving, not only taking. It is the kind of love the Lord has for us! The Bible talks about this kind of love in Romans 5:6: "You see, at just the right time, when we were still powerless, Christ died for the ungodly."

That is a radical statement of agape love. The Lord loved you when you were still partying and having sexual relationships with your boyfriends. When you were unconcerned with what God thought about your lifestyle, He loved you! That is the only solid basis for real love in a friendship, dating relationship, or eventually in a marriage.

Benefits Of Godly Relationships

I have seen the lives of many people shipwrecked because they bought Satan's lie that sexual involvement was the only way to meet their deep loneliness. Everyone has a desperate need to belong because they want someone to *know* them, and they have a great urgency to find someone who can take away the ache of loneliness. All too often *two* needy people find each other—both with the same need—and they try to meet that need in each other's life. The problem is that they really don't have anything to give. One day they finally realize they are bored and still lonely, but now they also feel cheapened and guilty.

The desire to share intimately and to belong are really not sinful. These are God-given needs. Trying to fulfill them sexually is where the hang-up lies. God wants us to experience an intimacy in our sharing that is non-sexual in nature. You have to make a choice to move beyond superficial relationships, those where you "shine on" the other person just to impress them.

Admitting that you really need someone can be frightening because all too often that is not seen as "having it all together." It means being willing to let someone into our heart enough to share our likes and dislikes, our strengths and weaknesses. It means being willing to receive love and give it, too. Sometimes that can hurt.

You may entrust your heart to someone who will hurt you, betray you, or step on something precious in your heart, but, believe me, *the risk is worth it*! Having a friendship with someone based on the agape love of Christ is a great experience.

There will be times when a friendship seems to be moving naturally into something more. Those "romantic vibes" start, and suddenly you are feeling more for someone than friendship.

That's when some important guidelines need to be set. It is important that you pray and think about these guidelines in advance. Resisting a tempting situation when you have determined your standards in advance is a lot easier than trying to make a decision when you are actually in the situation.

Dating is a time in life when you can learn the art of relating to the opposite sex. Eventually you get to know one certain person of the opposite sex in a way that prepares you for engagement and marriage.

I believe dating should be fun. When you first start dating someone, there will be those awkward moments when your tongue absolutely refuses to say what you want it to, your brain seems to go into neutral when it comes to conversation, and you feel like an idiot. That is normal and usually disappears quickly. Dating allows you opportunities to enjoy sports and activities together that will help you get to know each other better.

Dating is also a terrific way to get to know more about yourself. You learn how to *sense* the needs and feelings of another person and then how to *respond* to those needs and feelings. Good dating habits can fulfill that need for intimacy and companionship in a non-sexual setting.

If you don't take that kind of time in a relationship but instead give in to your sexual desires and become involved in heavy petting, you simply won't feel fulfillment. It is not God's plan. The Lord knows that nothing short-circuits a relationship and eliminates agape love faster than sexual exploitation, conquest, and focusing solely on the physical. Instead, it just intensifies the pain of loneliness.

Don't Date Unbelievers

Kristy was a young woman who had grown up in the church. She wasn't visually attractive, but she had a tremendous singing talent and an inner love for Christ. Kristy was always right in the middle of the action.

Everybody loved her, but she longed for a romantic relationship with a young man. I began noticing that she was absent from many of our single-adult events. When she did come, I could sense something distant about Kristy. Her eyes began to have a hard look about them. Slowly her dress and outward appearance began to change.

One day a young lady in our group told me that Kristy had been frequenting a gay bar. When I finally confronted her about it, she admitted that gay men were the only ones who really understood her. She said they would take her out and show her extravagant evenings on the town.

Kristy's parents and I both tried to reason with her about her dealings with unbelievers who were deceived sexually, but she hardened her heart. One day she announced that she was marrying a bisexual man! She said her boyfriend had prayed about his problem, and God had told him that what he was doing was okay. Kristy said, "If God can forgive him, so can I!"

For the next two years, this poor girl went through some of the most grueling sexual experiences and emotional pain I have ever heard of. One night, the young man finally walked out of her life for good. As far as I know, Kristy has never come back to the Lord.

What happened to that fine Christian young lady? I often considered her life while on my knees in prayer, and I've come to the conclusion that she wanted a man so badly that she was willing to pay any price to have her desire fulfilled. It began by turning away from God's people to hang out with Satan's crowd. This scenario is played out again and again in Christian families all over the world.

It is very important that the people you choose to date are Christians. You may know someone you would really like to date who is a non-Christian, but don't! Remember, one of the purposes for dating is to get to know someone in a way that can lead to engagement and marriage.

How many people have gone ahead and dated a non-Christian saying, "Well, we're not going to get married! After all, it's just a date!" only to find themselves in love and seeking ways to justify the marriage? It leads to tragedy, and God wants to spare you.

Your personal fellowship with Jesus is disrupted when you violate God's command and date a non-Christian. God still loves you and will continue to walk with you, but dating a non-Christian is sin. God makes that clear throughout the Bible. (See Deuteronomy 7:1-4 and 2 Corinthians 6:14-15.)

Dating should provide a mutual sharing on the deepest spiritual level. This is where intimacy takes place. Satan provides just the opposite—intimacy through sex—and it's a real rip-off.

The fulfillment in friendship—or in a dating relationship—comes as two people come together in Christ to share laughter, tears, caring, and sharing based around their mutual relationship with Jesus. Only there will you find a sense of belonging and the companionship you need.

Your relationship with God must come first. When it is right, the Lord can lead you into wonderful, exciting, fulfilling friendships and dating. God truly does want the very best for you.

Rich

1. Who gave you the desire to have intimate relationships?

2. Satan, the liar, has convinced this generation that the way to fulfill the need for intimacy is through _____ .

3. What is the name of the love that is the most needed in a relationship? How is that love different from other types of love?

4. It is much easier to resist a tempting situation when you have done what in advance?

5. Name four valid purposes for dating.

6. What is the number one "taboo" in choosing a dating partner?

Study these scriptures:

"The Lord God said, "It is not good for the man to be alone. I will make a helper suitable for him" —Genesis 2:18.

"So the man gave names to all the livestock, the birds of the air and all the beasts of the field. But for Adam no suitable helper was found. So the Lord God caused the man to fall into a deep sleep; and while he was sleeping, he took one of the man's ribs and closed up the place with flesh. Then the Lord God made a woman from the rib he had taken out of the man, and he brought her to the man. The man said, 'This is now bone of my bones and flesh of my flesh; she shall be called "woman," for she was taken out of man.' For this reason a man will leave his father and mother and be united to his wife, and they will become one flesh"—Genesis 2:20-24.

"When the Lord your God brings you into the land you are entering to possess and drives out before you many nations—the Hittites, Girgashites, Amorites, Canaanites, Perizzites, Hivites and Jebusites, seven nations larger and stronger than you—and when the Lord your God has delivered them over to you and you have defeated them, then you must destroy them totally. Make no treaty with them, and show them no mercy. Do not inter-marry with them. Do not give your daughters to their sons or take their daughters for your sons, for they will turn your sons away from following me to serve other gods, and the Lord's anger will burn against you and will quickly destroy you"—Deuteronomy 7:1-4.

"Flee from sexual immorality. All other sins a man commits are outside his body, but he who sins sexually sins against his own body. Do you not know that your body is a temple of the Holy Spirit, who is in you, whom you have received from God? You are not your own; you were bought at a price. Therefore honor God with your body"—1 Corinthians 6:18-20.

"Flee the evil desires of youth, and pursue righteousness, faith, love and peace, along with those who call on the Lord out of a pure heart"—2 Timothy 2:22.

"You see, at just the right time, when we were still powerless, Christ died for the ungodly"—Romans 5:6.

"Do not be yoked together with unbelievers. For what do righteousness and wickedness have in common? Or what fellowship can light have with darkness? What harmony is there between Christ and Belial? What does a believer have in common with an unbeliever?"—2 Corinthians 6:14-15.

"Do not rebuke an older man harshly, but exhort him as if he were your father. Treat younger men as brothers, older women as mothers, and younger women as sisters, with absolute purity"—1 Timothy 5:1-2.

"I would like you to be free from concern. An unmarried man is concerned about the Lord's affairs—how he can please the Lord. But a married man is concerned about the affairs of this world—how he can please his wife—and his interests are divided. An unmarried woman or virgin is concerned about the Lord's affairs: Her aim is to be devoted to the Lord in both body and spirit. But a married woman is concerned about the affairs of this world—how she can please her husband. I am saying this for your own good, not to restrict you, but that you may live in a right way in undivided devotion to the Lord"— 1 Corinthians 7:32-35.

PROMISCUITY
FROM A
MAN'S
POINT OF VIEW

6

WHAT ABOUT PROMISCUITY FROM A MAN'S POINT OF VIEW?

Dear Rich,

I am a Christian who has been very active at my church, and I love the Lord.

At work, the guys are really getting on my case because I have never had sex with a girl. They are putting a lot of pressure on me to take out someone "easy" so I can experience sexual intercourse. I have always been taught that it is wrong to have sex before marriage.

How can I get the guys off my back without doing something sinful? It doesn't seem right to have sex just to be one of the guys.

Jerry

Dear Jerry,

First of all, I understand your problem. As I crisscross this country speaking at conferences and in churches, I hear all the time about the peer pressure you are experiencing. Our society has become very *promiscuous* since the "free love" era began.

Promiscuity means to relax one's moral standards to the point that God's biblical standard of morality seems foreign to present day experience.

People like you, who are trying to live by the right and moral standards of God's Word, are made to feel silly and old-fashioned. Sticking by the morals of the Bible takes courage, and I know God is pleased with you for the decision you have made.

God is certainly not against sex. After all, He is the one who designed it in the first place! But in order to get the full pleasure out of it that God intends, you have to follow God's rules.

The purpose of sex is to join two people together to become one flesh. This means a lot more than joining together the physical anatomy of a man and woman. God wants to see two hearts join together in total commitment to one another in marriage. The oneness experienced by a husband and wife who are walking with God is unique and can never be duplicated outside the commitment of marriage.

Your friends are viewing sex as a conquest, and the only possible outcome of that is hurt, guilt, and empty exploitation. *God wants more for you!* He wants you to be able to enjoy the wonder of sex with the person He is preparing to be your mate. Anything short of that is settling for second best.

The Bible makes this very clear:

> My son, if sinners entice you, do not give in to them . . . do not go along with them, do not set foot on their paths; for their feet rush into sin. . . . But among you there must not be even a hint of sexual immorality, or of any kind of impurity, or of greed, because these are improper for God's holy people—Proverbs 1:10, 15-16; Ephesians 5:3.

The Lord wants you to be completely set apart for your mate so that you enter marriage holy and undefiled:

> It is God's will that you should be holy [sanctified]; that you should avoid sexual immorality; that each of you should learn to control his own body in a way that is holy and honorable, not in passionate lust like the heathen, who do not know God—1 Thessalonians 4:3-5.

God makes this command as simple as possible when He says, "Flee from sexual immorality" (1 Corinthians 6:18).

The Right Decision

One of my dearest friends is a minister by the name of Denny Duron. Denny is one of the finest Christians I have ever known. When he was only eighteen years of age he was preaching in some of America's largest churches.

Denny was a star athlete in college. In his senior year as quarterback at Louisiana Tech University, he took his team to a national bowl. Later he played professional football and also coached a college team. Never did he stop his constant travels as an evangelist.

During the entire time of this whirlwind lifestyle, Denny was single. He has always been an attractive person with an effervescent smile. Consequently, there seemed to be girls wherever Denny Duron went. But you could always trust Denny because he was much more in love with Jesus than he was with fame and acclaim. He kept himself pure and never allowed himself to be placed in a compromising position.

Denny never failed to share the love of Christ. Whether talking with a gas station attendant, a waitress, an alcoholic, a hurting teenager, or a divorced parent, the name of Jesus was always on his lips.

Several times during his single years, Denny stayed at our house. After he would leave, my wife would always comment on his pure conduct and exemplary life.

I'm sure some people wondered if Denny was destined to be single. But while he was keeping himself pure, God was preparing a perfect mate for Denny. During those years, a lovely young lady named Deanza Brock was also living for the Lord. When Denny was in his late twenties, he married Deanza, and today they are happily married with three beautiful children. Denny is still the finest preacher you would ever want to hear.

Whenever a young man asks, "What's the use of staying pure?" I tell them the story of Denny Duron.

You are making the right decision by waiting for marriage. Casual sex (going out with someone "easy," as you say, just to have sex to become one of the guys) is an insult to God's wonderful blessing on the sexual union He has for you in marriage.

Continue to do what is right. Your friends will see before long that they are not walking away from their immoral relationships unscarred. Sin *always* leaves scars. Having sex does *not* prove you are "a man."

When they begin to hassle you, don't give in to peer pressure. You are right! Pray that they will come to a real relationship with Jesus. Love them, and pray for them. But don't let their comments pressure you into sin. If they still refuse to respect your personal commitment to godliness, be courageous enough to find new friends.

Rich

Let's Review

1. What is the purpose for which God designed sex?
2. Only within the boundaries of what commitment can sex truly be enjoyed?
3. What should be our response as Christians toward sexual immorality?
4. Sin always leaves _____

Review these scriptures:

"Do not be misled: 'Bad company corrupts good character' "—1 Corinthians 15:33.

"Peter and the other apostles replied: 'We must obey God rather than men!' "—Acts 5:29.

"Adam lay with his wife Eve, and she conceived and gave birth to Cain. She said, 'With the help of the Lord I have brought forth a man' "—Genesis 4:1.

" 'Haven't you read,' he replied, 'that at the beginning the Creator "made them male and female," and said, "For this reason a man will leave his father and mother and be united to his wife, and the two will become one flesh"? So they are no longer two, but one. Therefore what God has joined together, let man not separate' "—Matthew 19:4-6.

"Marriage should be honored by all, and the marriage bed kept pure, for God will judge the adulterer and all the sexually immoral"—Hebrews 13:4.

"But among you there must not be even a hint of sexual immorality, or of any kind of impurity, or of greed, because these are improper for God's holy people"—Ephesians 5:3.

"My son, if sinners entice you, do not give in to them"— Proverbs 1:10.

"It is God's will that you should be holy; that you should avoid sexual immorality; that each of you should learn to control his own body in a way that is holy and honorable"—1 Thessalonians 4:3-4.

"I made a covenant with my eyes not to look lustfully at a girl"—Job 31:1.

"All the days of the oppressed are wretched, but the cheerful heart has a continual feast"—Proverbs 15:15.

See also Proverbs chapter 5, Proverbs 6:23-35, and Proverbs chapter 7.

PROMISCUITY FROM A WOMAN'S POINT OF VIEW

7

WHAT ABOUT PROMISCUITY FROM A WOMAN'S POINT OF VIEW?

Dear Rich,

My boyfriend and I have been dating for about a year now. I really love him, and we are planning to get married after I graduate from college.

Things between us are getting pretty heavy. He wants a more physical relationship, but I feel the Lord wants me to wait for marriage.

I really do love him, and we are planning to get married. Would it be so terrible for us to express our love for each other physically? I don't want to lose him.

Becky

Dear Becky,

Thanks for your letter and your honesty. God has much to say about love, marriage, and sex in His Word.

In our society, love and sex have become so intertwined that it seems nearly impossible to imagine a couple being in love without sexual involvement. People just assume they have a physical relationship.

Nothing could be further from what God intended. He designed sex for expressing love within the context of marriage—the commitment of husband and wife—not for selfish gratification outside of marriage.

The Bible is clear that extra-marital sex does not have God's blessing. The word used throughout Scripture is *fornication*, meaning sexual activity outside marriage. The Bible also says that "the body is not meant for sexual immorality, but for the Lord" and that we are to "flee from sexual immorality" (1 Corinthians 6:13,18).

Since it is clear what God says about sex outside of marriage, let me challenge you to rethink the issue of love. You say you and your boyfriend are in love and planning to get married when you finish school. Love is honestly wanting the highest good for someone. If you really do love your boyfriend, I challenge you to help him not to sin.

Spend some time talking about your desire to live in accordance with God's will, and then go together to the Lord and dedicate your relationship to Him. Spend time in the Word together. You will find the Lord showing you wonderful Scriptures to encourage and help you through the rough times. (You may want to start with 1 Corinthians 10:13.)

When Joseph faced the temptation of a sexual relationship with Potiphar's wife, his relationship with the Lord was what brought him through. He turned to her and said, "How could I do such a wicked thing and sin against God?" (Genesis 39:9).

Because Joseph had a love for God that was more important than anything else, he did not fall into the trap the devil and Potiphar's wife set for him. The same emphasis on your relationship with the Lord can see you through temptations.

Be wise enough to make sure you avoid situations in which there is opportunity for sexual activity. Be honest enough with each other to communicate when you are feeling vulnerable, and then love your boyfriend enough to help him avoid sinning.

A young woman who belonged to our fellowship had to learn this lesson the hard way. She had been raised in a Christian home and was truly a beautiful Christian lady.

During the course of our ministry, we had an evangelist come through our church. He had a fairly well-known ministry and was single. As soon as he met this woman, I could tell they had much in common.

In all honesty, I was hoping they would get together. They seemed perfect for each other. Whenever he came to town, he would spend the night with a family in our church. They would invite this woman over to their house after church. After everyone else went to bed, the two of them would stay up talking.

Even when he had a brief break in his ministry schedule, he would fly to our city to stay with the family. Each night he and the young woman would be left alone.

Finally, they became engaged. People everywhere talked about this fabulous couple. Wedding invitations were sent out, but then all of a sudden the man broke it off. The woman was crushed. Later in counseling we found out that the two of them had been doing more than talking. She said, "I should never have gone over to their house night after night. It was like we were setting ourselves up for a fall."

Now several years later they are both married. You don't hear much from him anymore, and she seems to be far from happy.

Oh yes, God is using both of them. But, apparently, if they had not gotten involved sexually, everything would have worked out for them. It all started because, as our friend said—they set themselves up for a fall.

Dating or engagement can be such a wonderful, fulfilling time of your life if you can walk with a clear conscience. Love each other enough to wait. Love each other enough to keep each other from sinning. You won't be sorry, and your walk with the Lord will reflect the blessings of righteousness.

You mentioned earlier the fear of losing your boyfriend if you don't have sex with him. If he is the man God has chosen for you, he will respect your moral standards and will also want to walk in the right path of the Lord. If he doesn't, let him go. The Lord will bring you the partner who is best for you, and you won't have to compromise your own spirituality to keep the relationship together.

Be strong enough to walk in obedience to the Scriptures, and you will know the wonderful, clean feeling of having a clear conscience before God. He really loves you!

Rich

Let's Review

1. What is the biblical word for sexual activity outside of marriage?
2. Name two practical goals of love.
3. Who was the young man in the book of Genesis who was greatly tempted?
4. What great benefit does the person who is morally pure enjoy?
5. If a young man truly loves a young lady, how will he act toward her physically?

Study these scriptures:

"Do you not know that we will judge angels? How much more the things of this life!"—1 Corinthians 6:3.

"No temptation has seized you except what is common to man. And God is faithful; he will not let you be tempted beyond what you can bear. But when you are tempted, he will also provide a way out so that you can stand up under it"—1 Corinthians 10:13.

"The coming of the lawless one will be in accordance with the work of Satan displayed in all kinds of counterfeit miracles, signs and wonders, and in every sort of evil that deceives those who are perishing. They perish because they refused to love the truth and so be saved"—1 Timothy 2:9-10.

"Flee from sexual immorality. All other sins a man commits are outside his body, but he who sins sexually sins against his own body"—1 Corinthians 6:18.

"Now Joseph was well-built and handsome, and after a while his master's wife took notice of Joseph and said, 'Come to bed with me!'

"But he refused. 'With me in charge,' he told her, 'my master does not concern himself with anything in the house; everything he owns he has entrusted to my care. No one is greater in this house than I am. My master has withheld nothing from me except you, because you are his wife. How then could I do such a wicked thing and sin against God?' And though she spoke to Joseph day after day, he refused to go to bed with her or even be with her. One day he went into the house to attend to his duties, and none of the household servants was inside. She caught him by his cloak and said, 'Come to bed with me!' But he left his cloak in her hand and ran out of the house.

When she saw that he had left his cloak in her hand and had run out of the house, she called her household servants. 'Look,' she said to them, 'this Hebrew has been brought to us to make sport of us! He came in here to sleep with me, but I screamed. When he heard me scream for help, he left his cloak beside me and ran out of the house' "—Genesis 39:6-15.

PORNOGRAPHY

8

WHAT ABOUT PORNOGRAPHY?

Dear Rich,

    A lot of the guys at work are really getting into pornography, and they say there is nothing wrong with it. They tell me sex is normal and that I'm a jerk if I don't join them.

    If God really did make sex, what's the big deal about looking at a few magazines? Is it really wrong for me to join in?

Rick

Dear Rick,

Pornography has always been a favorite pastime of young men everywhere. Unfortunately, it is creeping more and more into the private lives of this country's Christian men and women. You are not the only one facing this issue, so don't feel alone.

First of all let's define the word "pornography." The dictionary says, *"Pornography is the depiction of erotic behavior, as in pictures or writing, intended to rouse sexual excitement. It involves such things as books, photographs and film—all depicting erotic behavior intended to cause sexual excitement."*

A friend of mine related a story to me about this very problem. It had to do with a family in his church. The mom and dad were in their late thirties and financially very well off.

They had two sons, ages twelve and fourteen. Pampered and spoiled, the boys had the best of everything and were, quite honestly, "snobs."

The parents, although very successful in their business, were literally afraid of their sons and continuously tried to buy their love.

The family had my friend and his wife over to their home for dinner, and they showed them through the house. When they got to the bedroom of the fourteen year-old (remember this kid is only in the 9th grade), my friend and his wife were astounded to see pictures of naked women on his walls! Never once did the father comment on the pictures, apologize, or even offer an explanation. He acted as if it were perfectly normal.

Pornography is an issue that affects the whole family and concerns our entire value system. Fortunately, the Lord does give an answer to this dilemma.

You are right when you say God thought up sex in the first place, and He is the one who made sex enjoyable. It was God who placed sexual drives and appetites within you. Having sexual feelings and desires is not wrong. They only become problems when we step outside the protection of God's will.

Sex was intended by God to be the most intimate joining of a man and woman through the love and commitment that can only be found in marriage. Pornographic magazines and movies take this wonderful gift of God and turn it into something ugly. Abuse and violence are becoming more and more a part of this industry. Each year statisticians from an assortment of different secular and Christian magazines tell us that at least seven billion dollars is spent on pornography.

Each year between 100,000 and 500,000 American children will be molested. One in four girls will be molested or raped in this country before she reaches the age of twenty. Could there be a correlation between the amount of pornography sold and the amount of violent sexual acts and crime? I believe so!

Pornography also occurs on television and in the movies. In the April 1985 issue of *The Evangelist* magazine, Jimmy Swaggart reports:

Victor B. Cline conducted a revealing survey on the movies screened in theaters during a four-week period in a moderately conservative western city of 25,000. This city did not have any "porno" movie houses. The following is a summary of the sexual incidents, actions, and situations shown in the thirty-seven motion pictures screened during this period. (And don't forget, children were a part of the audiences.)

*Nudity—168 depictions
*Kissing, embracing, body contact—90 scenes
*Bed scenes with sexual connotations—49 scenes
*Dressing in undergarments with sexual context—36 scenes
*Verbalizing of sexual interest or intentions—36 scenes
*Caressing another's sex organs while clothed—27 scenes
*Caressing another's sex organs while nude—21 scenes
*Undressing—34 scenes
*Explicit intercourse—19 scenes

* Suggested or implied intercourse—17 scenes
* Homosexual activities—11 scenes
* Oral/genital intercourse—7 scenes
* Rape—4 scenes
* Obscene gestures—4 scenes
* Masturbation—3 scenes
* Sexual sado/masochism—3 scenes

Remember, this is today's "acceptable" public entertainment. And with such "normal" entertainment, is it surprising that pornographers must resort to the most shocking of perversions to jar the mental receptors—simply because pornography is being shown routinely over television, cable systems and in movies? (And let's not forget, children are viewing this.)

The emphasis is on what *you* get out of sex (rather than what two people *share*) and the attitude of "free sex"—whenever and with whomever it is available. All of this is directly opposed to what the Lord originally intended.

Filling your mind with these messages about sex can only leave you with the exploitive lies of the enemy rather than the joy of sex God intended. They are designed to arouse lustful feelings, which are then translated into sinful behavior.

In 1957, four nations, including the United States, Australia, New Zealand, and England relaxed their regulations on pornography.

Statistics show a dramatic increase in rape since that time in each of these countries. From 1957 to the present, rape is up 160 percent in Australia, 139 percent in the U.S., 109 percent in New Zealand, and 94 percent in England!

I don't know, Rick, how to make you better aware of the shocking long-term ramifications of pornography than to reprint part of Dr. James Dobson's January 1986 *Focus on the Family* newsletter titled, "Combatting The Darkness." Dr. Dobson served on the Attorney General's Commission on Pornography. He says,

> It is impossible to describe adequately what we witnessed during this term of governmental service. And yet, I wish our citizens understood. Most Christians seem to believe that pornography is characterized by air-brushed nudity in today's men's magazines. That *is* pornographic to be sure, but the industry has become far more perverse and wicked in recent years. Indeed, the *mainstream* of explicit material sold in sex shops today focuses on rape, incest, defecation, urination, mutilation, bestiality, vomiting, enemas, homosexuality and sadomasochistic activity.

Even child pornography, which is illegal and not available over the counter, continues to thrive in a multimillion dollar black market. It is produced by pedophiles for use by other pedophiles in the sexual exploitation of children. Obscenity is a wretched business, top to bottom.

But why *should* criminal law against pornography be enforced? Why should government object if some people want to amuse themselves with explicit materials? Is obscenity really a threat to society and to the individuals within it? You will hear those questions posed by television and newspaper reporters who clearly resent the work of our Commission. Let me respond for the record. Throughout this past year we have heard testimony from victims of pornography, from police officers, social scientists and concerned parents. Many of these witnesses have described the multiple harms associated with sexually explicit material. Let me list just a few of the pervasive dangers emerging from the evidence:

1. Depictions of violence against women are related to violence against women everywhere. The most cursory examination of the material being

marketed today makes it clear why that is true. I could not describe the offensiveness of these publications without being pornographic even in this context. Violent pornography also contributes to the so-called "rape-myth," leading men to believe that women really want to be abused even when they vigorously deny it.

2. The use of pornography seems to be addictive and progressive in nature. That is, those who get hooked on sexually explicit material tend to become obsessed by their need. It also interferes with the normal sexual relationship between husbands and wives.

3. The river of obscenity which floods our homes has reached the eyes and ears of children! Boys and girls are finding and viewing their parents' X-rated videos and magazines. They are also being bombarded by vile lyrics in rock music on radio, television and videos. Their morals are being corrupted by R-rated movies which dangerously link sex and violence. They are being shocked and titilated by obscenity on dial-a-porn phone lines. And on and on it goes. As a direct consequence, psychotherapists are seeing increasing

numbers of disturbed young patients who may never enjoy healthy attitudes about sex.

4. Pornography is degrading and humiliating to women. They are shown being beaten, hanged from trees, smeared with feces, urinated upon, and, of course, deprived of dignity and modesty. Men and boys are the purchasers of this material, using it primarily for masturbatory purposes. The entire female gender has reason to feel used and abused by this industry.

5. Pornography is often used by pedophiles to soften children's defenses against sexual exploitation. They are shown nude pictures of adults, for example, and told, "See, this is what mommies and daddies do." They are then stripped of innocence and subjected to brutalities that will be remembered for a lifetime.

6. Outlets for obscenity are magnets for sex-related crimes. When an adult bookstore moves into a neighborhood, an array of "support services" typically develops around it. Prostitution, narcotics and street crime proliferate. Ask anyone who lives near a sex shop. You'll hear an immediate protest.

7. So-called adult bookstores often become cesspools of disease and homosexual activity. The tiny video booths in these shops are used for private sexual behavior and become filthy beyond imagination. Holes in the walls between booths are provided for anonymous sexual encounters between adult males, etc. In this day of concern over AIDS and other sexually transmitted diseases, it is difficult to understand why local health departments have refused to close down these foul businesses.

8. Finally, pornography is damaging to the family in countless ways. We are sexual creatures, and the physical attraction between males and females provides the basis for every dimension of marriage and parenthood. Thus, *anything* that interjects itself into that relationship must be embraced with great caution. Until we *know* that pornography is not addictive and progressive . . . until we are *certain* that the passion of fantasy does not destroy the passion of reality . . . until we are *sure* that obsessive use of obscene materials will not lead to perversion and conflict between husbands and wives . . . then we dare not adorn them with the crown of respectability.

Society has an absolute obligation to protect itself from material that crosses the line established objectively by its legislatures and court system. That is not sexual repression; that is self preservation.

The Bible is clear when it says we are to "flee from sexual immorality" because our bodies are temples of the Holy Spirit. "You are not your own; you were bought with a price. Therefore honor God with your body" (1 Corinthians 6:18-20).

Feeding your sexual appetite with pornography can only lead to incredible temptation by Satan. God has called you to walk in the freedom of Christ—freedom to say "no" to sin, not "yes" to your friends.

Temptation is not sin. *Yielding* to temptation is sin. The Lord has always promised us that temptation will never be so strong we can't overcome it. Instead of filling your mind with the garbage of pornography, fill it with the truth of God's Word. The writer of Psalm 119 found the secret of overcoming sin when he said, "How can a young man keep his way pure? By living according to your word. . . . I have hidden your word in my heart that I might not sin against you" (Psalm 119:9,11). It will work for you, too.

Rich

Let's Review

1. Why does God condemn pornography?
2. What is pornography designed to do?
3. Temptation is not sin. What, then, is sin?
4. What is the secret to overcoming sin?

Study these scriptures:

"I made a covenant with my eyes not to look lustfully at a girl"—Job 31:1.

"Whatever is true, whatever is noble, whatever is right, whatever is pure, whatever is lovely, whatever is admirable—if anything is excellent or praiseworthy—think about such things"—Philippians 4:8.

"How can a young man keep his way pure? By living according to your word. . . . I have hidden your word in my heart that I might not sin against you"—Psalm 119:9, 11.

"We demolish arguments and every pretension that sets itself up against the knowledge of God, and we take captive every thought to make it obedient to Christ"—2 Corinthians 10:5.

"But I tell you that anyone who looks at a woman lustfully has already committed adultery with her in his heart"—Matthew 5:28.

SEXUAL FANTASY

9

WHAT ABOUT SEXUAL FANTASY?

Dear Rich,

Writing to you about my problem is really hard because I am embarrassed. But when I heard you speak, you seemed like someone who would understand.

I am a Christian and live a pretty clean life. But there is one area I can't seem to get control of: I always find myself dwelling on sexual things, and I can't get them out of my mind. When I meet someone I think is attractive, I wonder what it would be like to have sex with her.

God must be disgusted with me because I even have these thoughts in church. Sometimes I wonder if God even wants me after all this.

Is there anything you can say that will help me get my mind under control? I really hate myself when I have these thoughts!

Kenneth

Dear Kenneth,

Thanks for writing and being so honest about the trouble you are having with sexual fantasies. Believe me, you are not alone in this struggle. I think almost everyone fights the battle you are fighting at some point in their life.

When God designed sex, He intended it to bring pleasure and excitement. The problem is that we forgot to read His instruction book, the Bible, to find out when, how, and why sex has been given to us. God intended for sex to take place within the love and commitment of marriage. It was never meant to be used selfishly or casually, as it is today.

Because God did give you a sex drive, and because He wants you to wait until you are married to have a sexual relationship, He offers help within His Word regarding the sexual thoughts and fantasies you are feeling. Let's look into the Bible together and see what help God has to offer.

First, let me say that experiencing sexual *temptation* is not sin but simply a suggestion spoken into our minds by the enemy to activate our fleshly nature. Temptation does not become sin until we make a choice to accept and act upon it. When we yield to the temptation, however, we make a god out of our own sexual desires and appetites. The biggest problem is that we can't serve two gods. If you make your desires your god, then Jesus has to take second place. James 1:13-15 says it this way:

When tempted, no one should say, "God is tempting me." For God cannot be tempted by evil, nor does He tempt anyone; but each one is tempted when, by his own evil desire, he is dragged away and enticed. Then, after desire has conceived, it gives birth to sin; and sin, when it is full-grown, gives birth to death.

Can you see the progression? *Temptation* produces *immoral desire*. The devil does not want you to keep Jesus Lord of your life. He takes something God intended to be a wonderful blessing in your life (your sex drive) and turns it into something that activates your evil nature and drives a wedge between you and God.

Once the temptation has moved into immoral desire, it gives place to *sin*. The guilt, fear, and self-condemnation often keep us from wanting to come into God's presence. If the sin continues, eventually it brings spiritual *death*.

The apostle Paul knew about the war between his own sinful nature and walking in obedience. He clearly talks about the struggle in Romans, but he also gives the solution. "Who will rescue me from this body of death? Thanks be to God— through Jesus Christ our Lord" (Romans 7:24-25).

When the devil is spiritually attacking a person with the lusts of the flesh, it is foolish to fight back by physical means. Young adults are taught to counteract their sexual desire with exercise, busy schedules, or cold showers. These are all well-intentioned plans, but they are man's answer to a spiritual problem. We must fight spiritual attack with spiritual means. Answer these questions.

A. *What are you paying attention to?*

If you allow yourself to be impressed with the sensuality displayed on television, in movies, in magazines, and on the radio, then soon you will find yourself overwhelmed by lust. David said, "I will set no wicked thing before mine eyes" (Psalm 101:3, *KJV*).

B. *Is your heart and mind clean?*

Solomon said in Proverbs 4:23, "Above all else, guard your heart, for it is the wellspring of life." Jesus explained it even further in Mark 7:18-23:

> "Are you so dull? Don't you see that nothing that enters a man from the outside can make him unclean? For it doesn't go into his heart but into his stomach, and then out of his body. (In saying this, Jesus declared all foods clean.) What comes out of a man is what makes him 'unclean.' For from within, out of men's hearts, come evil thoughts, sexual immorality, theft,

> murder, adultery, greed, malice, deceit,
> lewdness, envy, slander, arrogance and
> folly. All these evils come from inside
> and make a man 'unclean.' "

A clean heart and mind will defeat Satan's temptation every time. David gave us the solution for keeping our hearts and minds clean when he said,

> How can a young man keep his way
> pure? By living according to your word.
> I seek you with all my heart; do not let
> me stray from your commands. I have
> hidden your word in my heart that I
> might not sin against you—Psalm
> 119:9-11.

C. *Do you love God more than your dating partner?*

The third way to fight sexual temptation is to have your priorities straight as far as your dating life is concerned. Jesus said, "Love the Lord your God with all your heart and with all your soul and with all your mind. This is the first and greatest commandment. And the second is like it: Love your neighbor as yourself" (Matthew 22:37-39).

If you'll love God first and foremost, He will help you to have the proper respect for yourself as well as others. When Christ's agape love rules your life and your choices, everyone is happy.

If you think cold showers are the answer to sexual temptation, then I challenge you to change your mind and start fighting this spiritual attack with the Sword of the Spirit, which is the Word of God.

The Bible says:

> No temptation has seized you except what is common to man. And God is *faithful*; he will *not* let you be tempted beyond what you can bear. But when you are tempted, he will also *provide a way out* so that you can stand under it— 1 Corinthians 10:13, *italics added*.

Our part is to be willing to look for the way out and then be willing to use it! We can't claim that the temptation was too strong to avoid or that we couldn't see a way around it. The Bible says there will be a way out and that God will not allow the temptation to be so strong that we are helpless. Seeing the way out and being willing to use it are *choices we have to make*.

You might be saying, "I don't know what it means when it talks about a way out." Let's be practical and honest for a minute. There are ways we actually set ourselves up to be tempted sexually. If you're reading pornography, God is not going to reach down and grab it out of your hand. Pornography is designed to arouse, and just having it in your possession is asking for trouble.

Perhaps certain books, movies, or television shows have arousing effects upon you. Most certainly, much of today's music carries a sexually suggestive theme. If you choose to read, watch, or listen to things that cause you problems, you have put yourself in a position where you should expect to be severely tempted. God expects us to use our heads and not give any ground to the enemy.

You see, the battle begins in the mind. What you allow your mind to entertain is what will determine your actions. In his second letter to the Corinthians, Paul speaks of our need to "take captive every thought to make it obedient to Christ" (2 Corinthians 10:5). This means filling our minds with God's Word instead of things that arouse. We must let the Word wash our minds of the suggestive thoughts brought by the enemy.

God Loves You!

You mentioned in your letter that you were afraid God was so disgusted with you that He probably didn't even want you anymore. *Nothing could be further from the truth. He loves you very much!* The reason He provides a way of escape, the reason the Lord encourages us to walk in purity even in our thoughts, and the reason Jesus died to provide us with forgiveness and free access to the throne room of God is because of His *wonderful love*.

127

The enemy will try any trick possible to keep a wedge between you and the Lord. His tricks are ugly. He is the one who presented you with the temptation, and now he is telling you how rotten you are for doing what he suggested you do in the first place! If the devil can keep you caught in the web of self-condemnation and guilt, you won't reach out to the Lord for the help and forgiveness He wants to give to you.

You don't have to turn spiritual cartwheels to get God to forgive you. The Bible says, "The sacrifices of God are a broken spirit; a broken and contrite heart, O God, you will not despise" (Psalm 51:17).

Take some time to be alone with the Lord, and tell Him honestly about the struggle you are having. Confess to Him that you have given in to the temptation of sexual fantasy, and then receive His forgiveness. He is anxious to comfort you. He really does love you.

Rich

1. What is it that tempts us according to James 1?
2. After sin is full-grown, what does it lead to?
3. Temptation produces what?
4. What often keeps us from wanting to come into God's presence?
5. Name five things that the devil can use to stimulate sexual fantasy in our lives.
6. Ultimately, where is the real battlefield when it comes to defeating sexual fantasy?

Study these scriptures:

"But I tell you that anyone who looks at a woman lustfully has already committed adultery with her in his heart"—Matthew 5:28.

"What a wretched man I am! Who will rescue me from this body of death? Thanks be to God—through Jesus Christ our Lord!"— Romans 7:24-25.

"When tempted, no one should say, 'God is tempting me.' For God cannot be tempted by evil, nor does he tempt anyone; but each one is tempted when by his own evil desire, he is dragged away and enticed. Then, after desire has conceived, it gives birth to sin; and sin, when it is full-grown, gives birth to death"—James 1:13-15.

"No temptation has seized you except what is common to man. And God is faithful; he will not let you be tempted beyond what you can bear. But when you are tempted, he will also provide a way out so that you can stand up under it"—1 Corinthians 10:13.

"We demolish arguments and every pretension that sets itself up against the knowledge of God, and we take captive every thought to make it obedient to Christ"—2 Corinthians 10:5.

MASTURBATION

10
WHAT ABOUT MASTURBATION?

Dear Rich,

   What do you think about masturbation? I can't find anything in the Bible that says it is wrong, but I still feel guilty. Can you help?

Rob

Dear Rob,

I am genuinely concerned with the movement in today's society that says masturbation is not only good and healthy but something that should carry no guilt with it. Sexual fantasy is wholeheartedly encouraged and even presented as a necessary precedent to a healthy sex life. I strongly disagree!

You are right in saying that the Bible does not speak directly about masturbation. There are no verses that say, "Thou shalt" or "Thou shalt not." However, the Word does contain some relevant principles, so let's look at them.

To see masturbation from God's perspective, we have to look at what He had in mind when He invented sex. Certainly He intended for us to enjoy the pleasure and fulfillment of the intimacy of a sexual relationship within the context of marriage. But God also had something even bigger and more wonderful in mind.

Paul wrote about that special design when he instructed husbands and wives in Ephesians chapter five. He told them,

> Wives, submit to your husbands as to the Lord. For the husband is the head of the wife *as Christ is the head of the church, his body,* of which he is the Savior. Now as the church submits to Christ, so also wives should submit to

their husbands in everything. Husbands, love your wives, *just as Christ loved the church and gave himself up for her* to make her holy, cleansing her by the washing with water through the word, and to present her to himself as a radiant church, without stain or wrinkle or any other blemish. . . . This is a profound mystery—*but I am talking about Christ and the church*—Ephesians 5:22-27, 32, *italics added*.

Marriage helps us understand the commitment of Christ to His Church and the Church to Christ. When you keep this firmly in your mind, how can the act of masturbation fit into God's sexual plan for your life? How can the intimacy, the trust, the giving love, and the security of sex with the woman your heavenly Father will bring to you in marriage ever compare with the physical lust-gratification you experience through masturbation?

The Lord longs to show you His love through sexual union with your future wife. Clouding that now with the emptiness, loneliness, and guilt masturbation brings leads you to the opposite conclusions. Masturbation is really an act of *sexual selfishness*.

The sin of masturbation (sexual release through self-stimulation) is really a person saying to God,

"I don't need a marriage partner or your provision for my life. I can fulfill my desires by myself."

This physical sexual sin only mirrors in the world a far greater problem in the spirit world. I call it "spiritual masturbation." Francis Schaeffer, the late Christian philosopher and theologian, once said, "If the Holy Spirit was taken out of your life and out of the world, would it make a difference in your Christian life?"

Many Christians would have to answer "no" to that question. Why? Because so many Christians today have learned how to go through the *motions* of fellowship with God without *knowing* God. They sing the right songs, know the right "catch words" in the church, and can go through the motions and form—without having God involved. They've learned the art of *religious self-stimulation*.

Renewing Your Mind

The Bible has some pretty strong things to say about sexual fantasy, and let's be honest and admit that *fantasy* is the controlling force in masturbation. Giving place to these scenes in your mind presents a foothold for the devil in the area of *lust*. Your mind is a war zone! Both the devil and the Lord want to be the focus of your attention. Satan will try everything possible to capture you through fantasy and then through guilt. So why give the devil the opportunity?

Look at 2 Corinthians 10:3-5:

> For though we live in the world, we do not wage war as the world does. The weapons we fight with are not the weapons of the world. On the contrary, they have *divine power to demolish strongholds.* We demolish arguments and every pretension that sets itself up against the knowledge of God, *and we take captive every thought to make it obedient to Christ—italics added.*

You see, the devil would like to make you believe that you are helpless because these are "just normal urges given to you by God." He would like to lure you into the trap of seeing sex predominantly as a necessary physical fulfillment of a natural instinct. Once our guards are down to the warfare going on, we fall to the temptations of lust and immorality. Our own inordinate affections become our god instead of the Lord Jesus.

We must take these verses seriously and take every thought captive. Our *minds* are our major sex organ! It all starts there, and that is where the Lord would have you fight and win the battle.

When a sexual battle begins in your mind, take it captive. Say, "No, Lord, I will not allow this thought to go any further! I can see that the enemy's plan is to lead me into sin, and I won't allow that to happen. So, Father, I bring this thought and give it to You. I want You in control of my mind, and I submit myself to You.''

Paul put it this way in Colossians 2:8: ''See to it that no one take you captive through hollow and deceptive philosophy, which depends on human tradition and the basic principles of this world rather than on Christ.'' Anyone or anything that pressures you into sexual sin ''because it is just a normal urge'' is luring you away from the plan God has for your life.

Your problem is not just the physical act of masturbation, it's now a spiritual problem. The decision you must make says, ''God, I need You now more than life. I commit my body, soul, and spirit wholeheartedly to You and refuse ever to go through the motions of a relationship with You without really knowing You again. I am Yours.''

When that commitment is made, God will help you have victory over this devil-motivated problem of masturbation. The Lord really loves you. He understands what you are struggling with and is right beside you to help get this area of your life under control. Let Him help!

Rich

1. What does marriage help us to understand?
2. In reality, what is masturbation?
3. What are the controlling forces in masturbation?
4. What is our major sex organ?

Study these scriptures:

"See to it that no one takes you captive through hollow and deceptive philosophy, which depends on human tradition and the basic principles of this world rather than on Christ"—Colossians 2:8.

"Wives, submit to your husbands as to the Lord. For the husband is the head of the wife as Christ is the head of the church, his body, of which he is the Savior. Now as the church submits to Christ, so also wives should submit to their husbands in everything.

"Husbands, love your wives, just as Christ loved the church and gave himself up for her to make her holy, cleansing her by the washing with water through the word, and to present her to himself as a radiant church, without stain or wrinkle or any other blemish, but holy and blameless"—Ephesians 5:22-27.

"Finally, brothers, whatever is true, whatever is noble, whatever is right, whatever is pure, whatever is lovely, whatever is admirable—if anything is excellent or praiseworthy—think about such things''—Philippians 4:8.

"For though we live in the world, we do not wage war as the world does. The weapons we fight with are not the weapons of the world. On the contrary, they have divine power to demolish strongholds. We demolish arguments and every pretension that sets itself up against the knowledge of God, and we take captive every thought to make it obedient to Christ''—2 Corinthians 10:3-5.

"But I tell you that anyone who looks at a woman lustfully has already committed adultery with her in his heart''—Matthew 5:28.

"Flee from sexual immorality. All other sins a man commits are outside his body, but he who sins sexually sins against his own body. Do you not know that your body is a temple of the Holy Spirit, who is in you, whom you have received from God? You are not your own; you were bought at a price. Therefore honor God with your body''—1 Corinthians 6:18-20.

HOW FAR
IS TOO FAR?

11

HOW FAR IS TOO FAR?

Dear Rich,

My fiance and I are so in love, I can't stand it! Both of us really love the Lord, but we also have this natural desire to express our love to one another. I'm really serious about this question. How far is too far? We know that going "all the way" is forbidden by God's Word, but the Bible is silent on many other areas that leave us with more questions than answers. We want to please God and express our love to each other. How far can we go?

Calvin

Dear Calvin,

I'm reminded of the time I was answering questions at a singles conference, and this same question came up. I looked at the young man and said, "Other than holding hands, anything below the neck is off-limits prior to marriage." The young man thought for a minute and then said, "Yeah, but what if we're standing on our heads?" The whole audience exploded into hilarious laughter.

Calvin, I can tell by your question that you love the Lord; however, you are obviously feeling more and more sensual love for your fiance. It's very important that you don't fall so in love with the girl that you fall out of love with Jesus. Please consider the following question:

Are you plain and simply *hot to trot?* By that I mean, is your love for this girl moving from a caring, happy friendship to a sensual one that keeps you meditating on sex day and night?

Prior to marriage, young couples are overwhelmed with the desire to discover new territories never before pioneered. This has to do with being young. The problem surfaces when couples begin to focus all of their exploratory activities on their fiance's body. Once their expedition begins, it is very difficult to turn back. One discovery leads to another. Pretty soon you realize that you're not in love—just hot to trot!

Let's discuss the activities that fall short of going "all the way." They are: *making out* (a term used to describe the act of longterm kissing, where arms and bodies are entangled with clothes on), *petting* (touching and fondling the partner's personal areas, i.e. the female's breasts and genitals and the male's genitals. Sometimes petting is accomplished while dressed, often times done while undressed), and *oral sex* (stimulating the genitals of the partner by oral—lips, tongue, mouth—means). These are the sexual activities that fall just short of sexual intercourse, and each one lights the fire for the next activity.

As a young man, there was a special girl whom I really liked, and I wanted to be with her. Whenever I'd sit next to her in class, I'd get really nervous. After finally becoming comfortable sitting next to her, I wasn't satisfied; now I wanted to hold her hand. After a couple of days, just holding hands between classes no longer satisfied me. Now I wanted to steal a kiss. I don't think I ever got enough courage to do that—I was only thirteen!

In an innocent way, I've tried to show you the dilemma young people experience when they get together. At every level there's a desire to take one more step. The young person who is driven to hold hands with his girlfriend will one day be driven to make out with her. They'll also be driven together to touch each others genitals and eventually engage in sexual intercourse.

Once a young adult lights the fire by having made out, they're going to be tempted to take the next step. It's natural. What am I saying? I'm saying that these activities I've mentioned—making out, petting, and oral genital stimulation—are activities known as "foreplay" to sexual intercourse and must be reserved for "the marriage bed!"

Someone has said, "Any activity that cannot be righteously satisfied is sin." *"Everything that does not come from faith is sin"* (Romans 14:23).

The apostle Paul said,

> Now for the matters you wrote about:
> It is good for a man not to marry. But
> since there is so much immorality, each
> man should have his own wife, and each
> woman her own husband—1 Corinthians 7:1-2.

God wants people to marry to avoid sinning. In other words, if we go God's way, our sexual desires will be satisfied and God will be pleased with our union.

Unconditional Love

Let me ask you another question, Calvin. Do you understand the meaning of *agape love?* If you really love your fiance, then all of the choices that you make toward her will be for *her* "highest good." Beyond choosing each others highest good, agape love is unconditional.

When you begin to consider a love that is unselfish and desires the best for your fiance, then premarital foreplay is out of the question. Never would a young man who truly loves a young lady risk her emotional health in order to fulfill his own lustful passions.

Besides, Calvin, "premarital foreplay" lights fires in the flesh that cannot be righteously satisfied. Sin enters the picture, and what started out as a happy friendship is now a miserable experience.

Look at what Solomon had to say about the way of the "strange woman":

> For the lips of an adulteress drip honey, and her speech is smoother than oil; but in the end she is bitter as gall, sharp as a double-edged sword. Her feet go down to death; her steps lead straight to the grave—Proverbs 5:3-5.

I'm not saying that your fiance is like this "strange woman" mentioned in Proverbs, but premarital foreplay (or sex) drives an individual into the depths of guilt and leaves them unsatisfied.

I suppose you already knew the answer, but maybe the problem really has to do with your question. Instead of asking, "How far is too far?" why not ask how far you can go into prayer and supplication? How far is too far with God? If that was your question, Calvin, I would answer, "There are *no limits* to reaching out to God in love." St. Paul said, "Oh, the depth of the riches of the wisdom and knowledge of God! How unsearchable his judgments, and his paths beyond tracing out!" (Romans 11:33).

If you and your fiance will motivate each other to reach out to God, then temptation will be changed back into natural God-given desires that will one day be fulfilled in marriage.

Rich

Let's Review

1. One of the keys to a dating relationship is that you don't let your love for Jesus be overwhelmed by your love for each other. Honestly now, how is it in your present relationship?

2. In this chapter we discussed three activities of "foreplay" that should be avoided before marriage. Name them.

3. It is natural for dating partners to want to go to the next level of physical affection after one level has been attained. How can this desire be defeated?

4. Complete this sentence: "Any desire that cannot be righteously satisfied is _____."

5. The highest form of Christian love is called _____ love, and it's goal for the other person is for his/her _____.

6. Where does the life of immorality lead, in general? (See Proverbs 5:3-5.)

7. The question you should really be asking is, "How far is too far with God?" Answer: There are no limits; you can go all the way!

Study these scriptures:

"Oh, the depth of the riches of the wisdom and knowledge of God! How unsearchable his judgments, and his paths beyond tracing out!"—Romans 11:33.

"Do you not know, brothers—for I am speaking to men who know the law—that the law has authority over a man only as long as he lives? For example, by law a married woman is bound to her husband as long as he is alive, but if her husband dies, she is released from the law of marriage'—Romans 7:1-2.

"Finally, brothers, whatever is true, whatever is noble, whatever is right, whatever is pure, whatever is lovely, whatever is admirable—if anything is excellent or praiseworthy—think about such things"—Philippians 4:8.

" 'Food for the stomach and the stomach for food'—but God will destroy them both. The body is not meant for sexual immorality, but for the Lord, and the Lord for the body"—1 Corinthians 6:13.

"Flee from sexual immorality. All other sins a man commits are outside his body, but he who sins sexually sins against his own body"—1 Corinthians 6:18.

"But among you there must not be even a hint of sexual immorality, or of any kind of impurity, or of greed, because these are improper for God's holy people"—Ephesians 5:3.

"We should not commit sexual immorality, as some of them did—and in one day twenty-three thousand of them died"—1 Corinthians 10:8.

"Treat younger men as brothers, older women as mothers, and younger women as sisters, with absolute purity"—1 Timothy 5:2.

"Flee the evil desires of youth, and pursue righteousness, faith, love and peace, along with those who call on the Lord out of a pure heart"—2 Timothy 2:22.

"But the man who has doubts is condemned if he eats, because his eating is not from faith; and everything that does not come from faith is sin"—Romans 14:23b.

"It is God's will that you should be holy; that you should avoid sexual immorality"—1 Thessalonians 4:3.

" 'If a man marries both a woman and her mother, it is wicked. Both he and they must be burned in the fire, so that no wickedness will be among you' "— Leviticus 20:14.

"Put to death, therefore, whatever belongs to your earthly nature: sexual immorality, impurity, lust, evil desires and greed, which is idolatry"—Colossians 3:5.

"Blessed are the pure in heart, for they will see God"— Matthew 5:8.

"I am jealous for you with a godly jealousy. I promised you to one husband, to Christ, so that I might present you as a pure virgin to him"—2 Corinthians 11:2.

"Everyone who has this hope in him purifies himself, just as he is pure"—1 John 3:3.

See also Proverbs chapter 5, 6:23-35, and chapter 7.

LIVING
TOGETHER

12

WHAT ABOUT LIVING TOGETHER?

Dear Rich,

My boyfriend and I are in college, and we are living together to conserve on expenses. It's really not as bad as it sounds because we have every intention of getting married, but we decided to wait until we are out of college. Besides, with all the marriages we see breaking up around us, we are a little scared. If we live together, we will know if our marriage will work. I don't want to be one of the divorce statistics. As long as we are committed to each other and not messing around or sleeping with anyone else, what is wrong with living together? Is God really so down on what we are doing?

Theresa

Dear Theresa,

Thanks for your honest letter. Living together has become more and more common, and the questions you ask are important. God does have some definite things to say about this in His Word, so let's look at His principles.

From the beginning of God's creation, He has intended for man and woman to be together. Since Adam could find no suitable helper among the animals he was naming, God said,

> "It is not good for the man to be alone. I will make him a helper suitable for him." So the Lord God caused the man to fall into a deep sleep; and while he was sleeping, he took one of the man's ribs and closed up the place with flesh. Then the Lord God made woman from the rib he had taken out of the man, and he brought her to the man—Genesis 2:18, 21-22.

Needless to say, man was thrilled with God's creation and has been finding fulfillment in woman ever since.

In the Garden of Eden there was no minister or justice of the peace to perform a wedding ceremony as we know it. The Lord was there, however, to place His stamp of approval on their commitment.

You mentioned in your letter that you were living together partly because of a fear of marriage, in light of those failing around you. I understand your concern, and it breaks my heart to see how divorce has infiltrated even Christian homes. *This was never God's will!* His will was to bring two people together in a loving, committed union that would last the rest of their lives. His will was for them to join together and become one, to uphold each other through the good times and the bad, and to walk transparently before each other and the Lord.

Unfortunately, sin entered the picture. The wonderful transparency God had intended broke down into an accusing, painful lashing out at one another and God. (See Genesis 3, especially verses 6-14.)

Living together without the commitment of marriage is settling for far less than God wants for your life. Written into these relationships is the spoken—or more often the unspoken—understanding that if things get too rough, you can simply split, with no strings attached. Let me guarantee you of something—things *will* get rough!

Every relationship, even one "made in heaven," goes through hard times, when quitting would be easier than pushing ahead and hanging in there until the problem can be worked through. The key is having Christ as the center of the relationship and remembering the commitment you made to each other—"until death do us part." You can pray and work it out. The option of divorce, or simply not living together any more, is taking the easy way out.

This is in complete opposition to what the Lord intended in marriage. His purpose was to give us a graphic example of Christ's love for the Church. (See Ephesians 5:22-33, especially verse 32.) Christ's love is agape love—unselfish, unconditional, and pure. His love reaches to us in complete commitment.

Nothing we can do will separate us from His love. He is completely and unreservedly loyal to us, always desiring the very best for us. This is the kind of love He wants to see in a marriage.

With this in mind, does your relationship contain that kind of commitment? All marriages have rough spots. But two people married in God's design will have that kind of commitment firmly implanted in their hearts as they walk together as husband and wife. Living together as a trial run for marriage is basing a relationship on all the wrong foundations and setting yourself up for failure.

Receive God's Best

You said you have every intention of marrying the man you are living with, so my question is, "Why haven't you?" If this is the man God has provided to be your marriage partner for the rest of your life, why wait? If, however, you are living together because you are somehow unsure about him—if that is the basis of your fear of becoming a divorce statistic—perhaps you had better do some serious praying and seek God's will in this matter.

The Word of God has made it clear that sex outside the commitment of marriage is *fornication*, which is plainly and simply sin. The Lord, through the inspiration of Scripture, has outlined our course of action. It leaves no loopholes. He says, "Let us purify ourselves from everything that contaminates body and spirit, perfecting holiness out of reverence for God" (2 Corinthians 7:1). This is not a suggestion—it is God's command.

He is not trying to pull an "authority trip" on you, (although He certainly does have the authority); neither is He trying to "rain on your parade." He honestly loves you so much that He wants only the best for your life. This is why He makes this command so firm. Living together can ultimately only bring you pain and a broken heart. Living together is sin, and it breaks the heart of God.

In respect for the God who loves you with agape love, and in respect for one another and your families, be obedient to God's Word. Decide if this is the man God intends for you to marry. If it is, separate for at least one month and purify yourselves from fornication. Spend this time in prayer and fasting (and repentance) and planning for the actual wedding day. This will help heal the wounds you've inflicted on each other as a result of your selfishness. Get your relationship started on the right track. After this period of time get married.

If your boyfriend is unwilling to go God's way, the swifter you break off the relationship, the better. Whichever you decide, do it *now*! The longer you postpone this decision, the more time you give the enemy and your own fleshly nature to talk you out of it. Choosing to continue the way you are now is actually making a god out of your relationship, the man you say you love, and your own desires.

> Now fear the Lord and serve Him with all faithfulness. Throw away [your] gods . . . and serve the Lord. But if serving the Lord seems undesirable to you, then choose for yourselves this day whom you will serve—Joshua 24:14-15.

The Lord loves you and wants the very best for you.

Rich

Let's Review

1. Living together as a trial run for marriage is basing a relationship on what?
2. What does the Bible call sex outside of marriage? What are the consequences which are sure to follow?
3. What is God's motive for not allowing premarital sex?
4. What will living together ultimately bring you?

Study these scriptures:

"Now fear the Lord and serve him with all faithfulness. Throw away the gods your forefathers worshiped beyond the River and in Egypt, and serve the Lord. But if serving the Lord seems undesirable to you, then choose for yourselves this day whom you will serve, whether the gods your forefathers served beyond the River, or the gods of the Amorites, in whose land you are living. But as for me and my household, we will serve the Lord"—Joshua 24:14-15.

"Do you not know that the wicked will not inherit the kingdom of God? Do not be deceived: Neither the sexually immoral nor idolaters nor adulterers nor male prostitutes nor homosexual offenders nor thieves nor the greedy nor drunkards nor slanderers nor swindlers will inherit the kingdom of God"—1 Corinthians 6:9-10.

"Flee from sexual immorality. All other sins a man commits are outside his body, but he who sins sexually sins against his own body. Do you not know that your body is a temple of the Holy Spirit, who is in you, whom you have received from God? You are not your own; you were bought at a price. Therefore honor God with your body"—1 Corinthians 6:18-20.

"But now I am writing you that you must not associate with anyone who calls himself a brother but is sexually immoral or greedy, an idolater or a slanderer, a drunkard or a swindler. With such a man do not even eat"—1 Corinthians 5:11.

"Since we have these promises, dear friends, let us purify ourselves from everything that contaminates body and spirit, perfecting holiness out of reverence for God"—2 Corinthians 7:1.

"I am afraid that when I come again my God will humble me before you, and I will be grieved over many who have sinned earlier and have not repented of the impurity, sexual sin and debauchery in which they have indulged"—2 Corinthians 12:21.

"For from within, out of men's hearts, come evil thoughts, sexual immorality, theft, murder, adultery"—Mark 7:21.

"Instead we should write to them, telling them to abstain from food polluted by idols, from sexual immorality, from the meat of strangled animals and from blood"—Acts 15:20.

"Marriage should be honored by all, and the marriage bed kept pure, for God will judge the adulterer and all the sexually immoral"—Hebrews 13:4.

"It is God's will that you should be holy; that you should avoid sexual immorality"—1 Thessalonians 4:3.

See also Genesis 3:6-14.

ABORTION

13

WHAT ABOUT ABORTION?

Dear Rich,

I am writing with a serious problem. My girlfriend Jenny has been seeing a man for most of this year. She is a Christian, but her boyfriend is not. She had been acting really weird for the last few days, and finally yesterday she told me what is bugging her. She is pregnant! She made me promise I wouldn't tell her parents, but she and this guy are talking about an abortion.

I don't think this is right, but she said not to try to talk her out of it. I can't just stand by and do nothing. Please, could you give me some advice about what I should say to her? Are there any verses in the Bible that say abortion is wrong? I don't want her to have an abortion.

Carmen

Dear Carmen,

I was really sorry to hear about your friend Jenny. To be single and facing what she has to deal with is more than any girl should have to go through. It certainly is not what God wanted for her life.

You did the right thing to write to me. Jenny is about to make one of the most important decisions of her life, and she needs help. You are a good friend to have recognized that and to have reached out for help.

It is alarming to note that each day 4400 babies are aborted in this country. That adds up to 1.5 million per year. Since 1973, over twenty million children have been aborted in the United States of America. That is an astronomical number of murders!

I don't know how else to say it, but abortion is the ultimate act of sexual immorality experienced between a man and a woman. What started out as the sin of fornication ends with the sin of murder. The reason why I say abortion is the ultimate act of sexual immorality is because a life is taken. It is true that lives are taken through sexual acts often in this country. But to take an innocent little life that has no means of resistance or protection, in my opinion, is sexual debauchery of the lowest kind.

I've even heard young women say, "I can't keep my baby, and I'd never give it away—so I'll kill it."

Abortion has become very controversial in the last few years. People are always arguing about the rights of the mother versus the rights of the unborn child. Although the Bible doesn't make a statement directly on abortion, it does contain some important scriptures that we need to look at.

The Bible mentions children as people before they are born. It always makes the presumption that from the moment of conception, the life inside the mother is a person. In Psalm 139:13-16, the Bible shows how involved God was with David before he was ever born:

> For you created my inmost being; you knit me together in my mother's womb. I praise you because I am fearfully and wonderfully made; your works are wonderful, I know that full well. My frame was not hidden from you when I was made in the secret place. When I was woven together in the depths of the earth, your eyes saw my unformed body. All the days ordained for me were written in your book before one of them came to be.

Isaiah later wrote, "Before I was born the Lord called me" (Isaiah 49:1). God told Jeremiah, "Before I formed you in the womb I knew you, before you were born I set you apart; I appointed you as a prophet to the nations" (Jeremiah 1:5).

The apostle Paul wrote in the New Testament, "But when God, who set me apart from birth . . . " (Galatians 1:15). When Mary, who was pregnant with Jesus, came to her Aunt Elizabeth's home, the Bible says Elizabeth spoke to her, "As soon as the sound of your greeting reached my ears, the baby in my womb leaped for joy" (Luke 1:44). The baby, who was to become John the Baptist, responded to the Messiah within Mary's womb.

These references make it clear that God sees a baby as a person from the moment of conception. He has planned the course of their lives even before they are born.

Countless scriptures in the Bible call on the "people of God" to rescue the fatherless and the innocent. Here are a few verses you can look up:

Exodus 22:22
Exodus 23:7
Psalm 10:8
Psalm 10:14
Psalm 22:3
Psalm 94:6, 20-23
Proverbs 6:16-17
Proverbs 24:11-12
Jeremiah 7:6
Jeremiah 22:3

As shocking as this statement may seem, I believe it with all of my heart: Abortion in these days is even worse than in the days of Herod, Pharaoh, and Hitler.

Judgment is coming. I believe that we here in North America will live to see as many people die with the AIDS plague as killed by abortion! What started out as a "party" has turned into a "wake."

Alternatives To Murder

Since, as we have seen, the baby within your friend is a person right now—and God has a plan for his or her life—to abort that baby is, in fact, *murder!* God has made it very specific in the Ten Commandments, as well as other places in Scripture, that murder is sin. Abortion is not an option, it is murder. What, then, are the options for your friend?

It may not be possible for your friend to keep her baby. Parenting is a huge responsibility even when you have two mature parents with a stable marriage and a reliable income. But many would-be parents would give almost anything for a baby to adopt. Due to the legalization of abortion, better birth control methods, and more unwed mothers keeping their babies, would-be parents often have to wait years for a child of their own. Many adoption agencies will not even accept new applications.

Couples who try to adopt really want a baby. They can offer the love, security, and home atmosphere every child needs. Jenny can have the assurance of knowing her baby is with parents who wanted a baby so badly they were willing to go through a long process to become adoptive parents.

Perhaps the reason Jenny and her boyfriend are seriously considering abortion is because they feel they are not ready to have a child of their own; or maybe they don't want anyone to know Jenny is pregnant. Abortion seems like the easy answer.

I pray they stop and realize the consequences of their actions. I counsel with girls all the time who have had an abortion, and even years later they are still suffering incredible guilt and remorse. The enemy may sell the idea of abortion as a simple, painless solution, but he is lying. He will accuse, bring guilt, and often even try to turn Jenny from the Lord because of this big secret she has to keep hidden. It is not an easy answer but one with long-range consequences.

Admitting their wrong to their parents and having others know she is pregnant will not be easy. But for the immorality Jenny and her boyfriend became involved in, this is one of the consequences. Deciding to "bite the bullet" now and go through with the pregnancy won't be a picnic, but it is the only responsible decision for them to make. Covering up one sin with another will only make matters worse.

Thinking of the child—instead of themselves— is necessary now. That baby is a child, formed and fashioned by God, with a purpose and plan for his or her life. Is nine months of embarrassment worth the taking of a baby's life? I am positive that God doesn't think so!

Many agencies can help Jenny. Our ministry is associated with *SAVE THE BABY*, an organization designed to help girls like Jenny. These kinds of organizations offer a variety of services. I would like to talk with Jenny personally and put her in touch with people who can help her. She can call our ministry *twenty-four hours a day* at our crisis line—(206) 756-5333. Someone will always be there to care and help (as well as pray with) Jenny and her boyfriend. Please encourage her to call.

Rich

Let's Review

1. God sees a baby as a person beginning when?
2. The truth is that abortion is _____.
3. What is the only responsible, loving, unselfish decision that Jenny and this boy can make?
4. What is one of the results that a woman suffers when she has had an abortion?
5. Sin always has its _____.

Study these scriptures:

"You shall not murder"—Exodus 20:13.

"For you created my inmost being; you knit me together in my mother's womb. I praise you because I am fearfully and wonderfully made; your works are wonderful, I know that full well. My frame was not hidden from you when I was made in the secret place. When I was woven together in the depths of the earth, your eyes saw my unformed body. All the days ordained for me were written in your book before one of them came to be"—Psalm 139:13-16.

"Listen to me, you islands; hear this you distant nations: Before I was born the Lord called me; from my birth he has made mention of my name"—Isaiah 49:1.

"Before I formed you in the womb I knew you, before you were born I set you apart; I appointed you as a prophet to the nations"—Jeremiah 1:5.

"Rescue those being led away to death; hold back those staggering toward slaughter. If you say, 'But we knew nothing about this,' does not he who weighs the heart perceive it? Does not he who guards your life know it? Will he not repay each person according to what he has done?"—Proverbs 24:11-12.

"As soon as the sound of your greeting reached my ears, the baby in my womb leaped for joy"—Luke 1:44.

"The Lord is close to the brokenhearted and saves those who are crushed in spirit. A righteous man may have many troubles, but the Lord delivers him from them all; The Lord redeems his servants; no one who takes refuge in him will be condemned"—Psalm 34:18-19, 22.

Recommended Reading

1. Allen, Ronald B., *Abortion: When Does Life Begin?* (Multnomah Press: Portland, 1984).
2. Brand, Dr. Paul W.; Yancy, Philip, *Fearfully and Wonderfully Made* (Zondervan Publishing House: Grand Rapids, 1980).

3. Koop, C. Everett; Schaeffer, Francis A., *Whatever Happened to the Human Race* (Good News Publishers/Crossway Books: Westchester, IL, 1983).
4. Powell, John, *Abortion (The Silent Holocaust)* (Argus Communications: Allen, Texas, 1981).
5. Reagan, Ronald, *Abortion and the Conscience of the Nation* (Thomas Nelson: Nashville, 1984).

HOMOSEXUALITY

14
WHAT ABOUT HOMOSEXUALITY

Dear Rich,

I have a problem that is hard to talk about. I am afraid to tell anyone, but I thought you might be able to help me.

You see, I am a homosexual. I first started to know this when I was in junior high. I wasn't interested in girls, and I would wake up having dreams about guys. I didn't tell anyone because I was afraid of being called a fairy or a faggot.

Now that I am in college, my attraction to guys is getting even stronger. I told my best friend, and he said I should buy some pornography to try and get interested in girls. I did, but it didn't help.

Rich, I am a Christian, and I don't want to stop being one; but what can I do? If I was born this way, how can I ever expect to change? I am the way I am, right? Write me back.

Brad

Dear Brad,

It took a lot of courage to write me as honestly as you did, and I respect you for doing so.

Let me see if I can address a few of your concerns. You mentioned in your letter that you are a homosexual and that you felt you had no choice in the matter because you were born that way. Let me state as strongly as I can: *There is hope*!

In all of the major studies done by researchers, no one has been able to prove in any way that sexual preference (homosexuality, bisexuality, or transexuality) is passed on through genetics. Many have tried, looking for a way to explain homosexual behavior (or more often attempting to justify it), but not one conclusive piece of evidence has been found.

On the contrary, the Bible teaches that just the opposite is true. Consider 1 Corinthians 6:9-11:

> Do you not know that the wicked will not inherit the kingdom of God? Do not be deceived: Neither the sexually immoral nor idolators nor adulterers nor male prostitutes nor homosexual offenders . . . will inherit the kingdom of God. And that is what some of you were. But you were washed, you were sanctified, you were justified in the name of the Lord Jesus Christ and by the Spirit of God.

Did you catch that? That is what some of you *were*! This implies that change is not only possible but available to you through what the Lord Jesus Christ did on the cross! It isn't even logical to assume that God would refuse to allow someone into His Kingdom for something he had no control over!

In other words, all of God's laws are rooted in unconditional love. His laws are for our protection. They are also reasonable laws, and that means they are possible to attain. God's love would not allow Him to produce a law that we could not keep and then send us to hell for not keeping it. That would be unreasonable.

You didn't say in your letter whether you have been involved in a homosexual relationship. It really doesn't matter, however, because homosexuality (as does any sexual sin) gets its most damaging hold *in the mind.* Jesus addressed this when He gave the Sermon on the Mount. I realize the verse here deals with heterosexual adultery, but the truth is the same. "You have heard that it was said, 'Do not commit adultery.' But I tell you that anyone who looks at a woman lustfully has already committed adultery with her in his heart" (Matthew 5:27-28).

Jesus was pointing out that sin is not just the act. It is the whole thought process that leads you to the place of the act. Reading pornography in order to try to feel heterosexual feelings is *not* the answer. Being free from homosexuality is not simply exchanging same-sex lust for opposite-sex lust. God wants to deal with the lust . . . period.

Because of the death and resurrection of Jesus, He offers us forgiveness and *freedom from sin,* which must start with a transformation of the mind. The first step to freedom is confessing the lust and sexual appetite to the Lord. He will not condemn you but instead stands waiting eagerly to put an arm of forgiveness and comfort around you. Acknowledging your need before God is the starting point to complete freedom from homosexual lust and behavior.

Many circumstances in your life have left you vulnerable to homosexual temptations. Past hurts and maybe even some sexual abuse in your own life have given this conflict a foothold. Although these experiences are almost impossible to address in a letter, there are ministries all over the country whose specific calling from the Lord is to help people walk away from homosexuality. The main office and referral center for these Christian ministries and support groups is EXODUS INTERNATIONAL, P.O. Box 2121, San Rafael, CA 94912.

The enemy would love to continue telling you there is no way out and that you are hopelessly trapped in homosexuality for the rest of your life. *That is not true.* There is help in Jesus. Yes, there will be a process of making right choices. The Bible says we are to resist the enemy, take captive every thought, and make it obedient to Christ. (See 2 Corinthians 10:3-5.)

The Lord is not asking you to do something that is impossible. You will struggle against sin and the flesh, and some healing will be needed; but the Lord can and will see you through!

I have enclosed a recommended reading list to help you replace the lies of the enemy with the truth of Christ. With the Lord's help and your cooperation, you really can see the devil defeated in this area of your life. God bless you!

Rich

Let's Review

1. If the homosexual desire is not genetic or inherited, what is the root of homosexuality?
2. Where is the key battleground for defeating homosexual desire?
3. Are God's laws reasonable?
4. What is Satan's constant lie to the person struggling with homosexuality?

Study these scriptures:

"For though we live in the world, we do not wage war as the world does. The weapons we fight with are not the weapons of the world. On the contrary, they have divine power to demolish strongholds"—2 Corinthians 10:3-5.

"Do not lie with a man as one lies with a woman; that is detestable"—Leviticus 18:22.

See also Genesis chapter 19 and Romans chapter 1.

Recommended Reading

1. Field, David, *The Homosexual Way—A Christian Option?* (InterVarsity Press: Downers Grove, Illinois, 1979).
2. Lovelace, Richard, *Homosexuality, What Christians Should Know About It* (Fleming Revell Co.: Old Tappan, NJ, 1984).

3. Payne, Leanne, *The Broken Image* (Crossway Books: Ill., 1981).

4. White, John, *Eros Defiled* (InterVarsity Press: Downers Grove, Ill., 1977).

5. Worthen, Frank, *Steps Out of Homosexuality* (Love in Action: San Rafael, 1984). Write directly to Love in Action, P.O. Box 2655, San Rafael, CA 94912.

INCEST

15

WHAT ABOUT INCEST?

Dear Rich,

This is a hard letter for me to write. I wanted to talk with you after you spoke today, but I was afraid someone else would hear.

You see, my father sexually abused me from the time I was twelve years old until I left home two years ago. I am afraid that if I tell anyone they won't believe me and my dad will get mad. I don't know what he would do.

I tried to tell my mom once that I didn't like to have Dad touch me, but she said I was just being silly. She said he loved me and liked to give me hugs to show it. She doesn't know what used to happen when she left for work at night and Dad would come into my bedroom. If he loved me, how could he do what he did?

A man asked me out on a date last week. I really wanted to go, but I knew if he ever found out, he wouldn't like me. So I said, "No."

189

I'm trying to be a good Christian, and I read my Bible and pray sometimes. But it's hard to believe that the Lord loves me after having allowed my father to do what he's done. What should I do?

Sue

Dear Sue,

My heart broke when I read your letter. I could feel in your words the hurt you have experienced, and I thank you for being honest with me about this problem in your home.

This is not a new problem in society. In fact, there are ten recorded cases of incest in the Bible. They include:

1. Lot and his two daughters (Genesis 19:30-36)
2. Abraham and Sarah* (Genesis 20:11-13)
3. Nahor and Milcah* (Genesis 11:27-29)
4. Reuben and Bilhah (Genesis 35:22; 49:3-4)
5. Judah and Tamar (Genesis 15:-18; 1 Chronicles 2:3-4)
6. Amram and Jochebed (Exodus 6:20)
7. Amnon and Tamar (2 Samuel 13:8, 11-14)
8. Absolom and David's wives (2 Samuel 16:21-22)
9. Herod and Herodias (Matthew 14:3-4; Mark 6:17-18; Luke 3:19)
10. The unnamed Corinthian man described by Paul in 1 Corinthians 5:1

*(It should be noted that such marriages as those of Abraham and his half-sister Sarah, and that of Nahor and Milcah, occurred before the Levitical Law was given. They were, therefore, not technically sin. See Acts 17:30.)

Sue, you *do* have a right to see this relationship with your father stop. *This is not right,* and you do not have to continue letting him abuse you. You are precious in God's sight, and this is not His will for your life. Since you said that you have moved out of the house, I assume this problem has ended.

As hard as it may be, you need to tell someone you can trust. You need to tell your mother, a friend, or your pastor; and you need to *keep* telling them until they believe you. Their reaction at first may be one of shock, as no one likes to believe a father would do this to his daughter. That doesn't mean it is your fault, however, or that they don't believe you. If you can't find an adult you can trust at home, work, or church, then you need to call our twenty-four hour prayer line at 206-756-5333.

It's important that you don't just wait and hope things will get better. They probably won't. The Lord does not want you to be hurt any longer. So keep telling someone until you get help.

What your father has been doing to you is *wrong.* Incest is strictly forbidden in Leviticus chapter eighteen, and your father needs help. Telling a friend who can help will not only be the best thing for you, but it will also get your father the help he needs.

The problem you have asked about not only happens to young girls but to young boys as well. I don't want you to think that you are the only one or that this is solely a female problem.

Part of your letter especially touched me. You said that you feel no man would ever love you if he knew about the kind of relationship you have had with your father. That is *not true*! You have been a victim of sin—the confused way of thinking in your father's mind. That does not mean you are ugly, dirty, or bad.

The Lord wants to heal the hurts deep inside you and make you into a beautiful woman of God. Sometimes the people who have been hurt the most are the same people God can use later to help bring healing to someone else.

Do you know how Jesus sees you right now? He sees a hurt little girl who is frightened and emotionally bruised. He longs to reach out and take you in His arms (His touch never hurts!) and let you snuggle close. He will heal all those places that seem so hurt now. While Jesus is healing you, He will make you into a beautiful woman. And He will bring you a husband, in just the right timing, who will love you for who you are—a daughter of the King!

Let Jesus comfort you, and let Him free you from this relationship with your father by leading you to someone you can tell—someone who can help you.

Jesus loves you!

Rich

Let's Review

1. What are some of the biblical examples of incest?
2. What is the first thing the victim of incest needs to do?
3. Should you wait and hope things get better before you do anything about the one abusing you?
4. Can a person ever expect to be free of this wound? How?

Study these scriptures:

"He said, 'If you listen carefully to the voice of the Lord your God and do what is right in his eyes, if you pay attention to his commands and keep all his decrees, I will not bring on you any of the diseases I brought on the Egyptians, for I am the Lord who heals you' "—Exodus 15:26.

"He sent forth his word and healed them; he rescued them from the grave"—Psalm 107:20.

"But he was pierced for our transgressions, he was crushed for our iniquities; the punishment that brought us peace was upon him, and by his wounds we are healed"—Isaiah 53:5.

"But for you who revere my name, the sun of righteousness will rise with healing in its wings.

And you will go out and leap like calves released from the stall''—Malachi 4:2.

"Jesus answered, 'It is written: "Worship the Lord your God and serve him only." ' ''—Luke 4:8.

"Cast all your anxiety on him because he cares for you"—1 Peter 5:7.

See also Exodus chapters 18 and 20.

VENEREAL
DISEASE

16

WHAT ABOUT VENEREAL DISEASE?

Dear Rich,

Do you think diseases like Herpes and AIDS are really God's way of punishing immoral people and homosexuals?

Scott

Dear Scott,

Sexually transmitted diseases, more commonly known as venereal disease or V.D., have been a problem in society for a very long time. They have recently come to the forefront of our thinking, however, because of the rapid spread of the incurable herpes and AIDS.

None of these diseases are found only within a certain community of people, like the homosexuals. It was first thought only homosexuals contracted AIDS, but the disease has now spread into the general population as well. But where did it begin—with actively homosexual men with several lovers (85%); intravenous drug users (10%); or Haitian refugees (5%)?

In answer to your question, most certainly the Lord is grieved with the promiscuity in our society that has turned V.D. into a national epidemic. Casual sex and changing sexual partners as often as socks is far from God's intention! His purpose in creating the enjoyment of sex was to enrich oneness in the relationship between a husband and wife.

Man and Satan have taken God's beautiful gift and warped and distorted it until sex has become a god to our pleasure-seeking society. When God's laws are broken, consequences must be paid.

Chapters one and two of Romans talk about the cost of sin. Although this passage speaks predominantly of homosexual sin, the Lord's principle applies to all other sexual sins as well. Perhaps the current outbreak of AIDS, herpes, and other venereal diseases are not curses sent from God on individuals as much as natural consequences of their sin. They are reaping what they have sown. Romans 1:27 says they have "received in themselves the due penalty of their perversion."

When the Lord inspired the writing of His laws in what we have come to know as the Bible, He carefully outlined what we should and should not do. Going against those laws is like buying a model airplane, throwing away the instructions, and assembling it "our way." When the model doesn't go together right, we get frustrated and eventually throw it away in disgust.

God was our creator/inventor, and He knows how we will best operate. He wrote the instruction manual (the Bible), and if we follow its instructions, we will operate smoothly. We will be happy and fulfilled because we have followed His guidance.

When we refuse to accept God's will and choose instead to go our own way, the Lord will not stop us. He will weep for us, spend time in intercession before the Father for us, and do all He can to bring us to repentance. But He will not violate our free wills. Walking our own way has its consequences, and they are often painful.

The "sexual revolution" of today may bring momentary pleasure, but the consequences are devastating. A moment of sexual pleasure is hardly worth the cost when followed by lifelong pain and embarrassment or even death from venereal disease.

"Great peace have they who love your law, and nothing can make them stumble. . . . All your commands are trustworthy" (Psalm 119:165,86).

Scott, you must understand that God's laws are loving laws. He has given us boundaries. Within those boundaries there is great peace. He is not against us enjoying life to the fullest, but He is against Satan's desire to steal from us, destroy us, and kill us.

God is against Satan's desire to inflict us with disease. But for God to keep us full of life, He needs our cooperation. If you will purpose in your heart to live within His boundaries, then you will know what *abundant life* is all about.

Rich

Let's Review

1. When God's laws are broken, what are the consequences to be paid?
2. What is God's instruction manual that tells how to operate our lives with success and peace?

Study these scriptures:

"In the same way the men also abandoned natural relations with women and were inflamed with lust for one another. Men committed indecent acts with other men, and received in themselves the due penalty for their perversion"—Romans 1:27.

"Do not be deceived: God cannot be mocked. A man reaps what he sows"—Galatians 6:7.

See also Romans chapters 1 and 2, and Psalm 165.

Scriptures dealing with God's blessings that come from keeping His laws:

"Blessed is the man who does not walk in the counsel of the wicked or stand in the way of sinners or sit in the seat of mockers. But his delight is in the law of the Lord, and on his law he meditates day and night. He is like a tree planted by streams of water, which yields its fruit in season and whose leaf does not wither. Whatever he does prospers"—Psalm 1:1-3.

"Praise the Lord. Blessed is the man who fears the Lord, who finds great delight in his commands. His children will be mighty in the land; each generation of the upright will be blessed. Wealth and riches are in his house, and his righteousness endures forever"—Psalm 112:1-3.

See also Psalm 91.

ORAL SEX

17

WHAT ABOUT ORAL SEX?

Dear Rich,

I've been going with a young lady for about eight months, and we really believe that we're in love. We don't want to have sexual intercourse because we know that would be a sin and hurt God. We have been looking for alternative ways to show each other how much we love one another.

Some of our friends have been talking about oral sex. It's very popular. We love each other so much that we're willing to do anything to prove it. Like I said before, though, we are Christians and feel that intercourse before marriage is out of the question. What do you think about "oral sex," Rich?

Fred

Dear Fred,

This is a very difficult question to deal with because it has brought about such division in the Christian Church. Some people believe that the act of oral sex is an abomination. Others believe that this activity is just another part of the act of love in marriage.

First of all, let me explain what oral sex is. Oral sex is stimulating the genitals of one's partner through oral means (lips, tongue, or mouth).

More and more young couples believe that oral sex is a way for them to be sexually gratified prior to marriage without loosing their virginity. They don't want to lose their virginity because they feel that there is something extra holy about keeping it. They believe God will be pleased with them.

To be quite honest, the Bible is silent on this subject. If it was a sin, God would strictly forbid it in marriage. Therefore, we may assume that oral sex can be part of the love-making process within the boundaries of holy marriage, if both husband and wife are in agreement.

On the other hand, oral sex, making out, petting, and intercourse would have to fall into the category of fornication if done outside of marriage. Each one of these activities leading up to intercourse is called "foreplay" and *lights the fire* for the next activity. Once you light the fire in foreplay, there is no way that you can righteously fulfill your desires outside of marriage.

Oral sex outside of marriage is a sin, and it breaks God's heart. I'm astounded by stories that I've heard about Christian parents who have counselled their teenagers to have oral sex because it's not as bad in God's eyes as going "all the way." This kind of reasoning suggests that our great God is something less than a moron.

The devil has duped many Christians with the lie that says we must have an alternative for sin. Christian teenagers love the word "alternative." We have religious rock now as an alternative to secular rock. We have religious discos, theaters, and nightclubs. *These alternatives just drag us closer and closer to the real thing.*

When a person comes to Christ, they lay their sin, their desires, and their needs at the feet of Jesus. At that point that person becomes a love-slave to Jesus Christ. He or she is no longer looking for alternatives to gratify old fleshly lusts; instead they're looking for the "will of God."

Fred, this topic has not been an easy one to deal with. I encourage you to serve God wholly in this matter. If you're looking for alternatives to sexual intercourse, fall in love with Jesus. If you'll commit yourself completely to Christ and remain pure, He'll grant you a great wife. Then you won't need an alternative because you'll have God's will.

Rich

Let's Review

1. Can oral sex be a part of a Christ-centered marriage?

2. Like "making out," "petting," and "intercourse," oral sex must be considered _____ if done outside of marriage.

3. What is one of the devil's great lies that he tells many Christians?

Scriptures dealing with immorality:

"Do you not know that the wicked will not inherit the kingdom of God? Do not be deceived: Neither the sexually immoral nor idolaters nor adulterers nor male prostitutes nor homosexual offenders nor thieves nor the greedy nor drunkards nor slanderers nor swindlers will inherit the kingdom of God. And that is what some of you were. But you were washed, you were sanctified, you were justified in the name of the Lord Jesus Christ and by the Spirit of our God"—1 Corinthians 6:9-10.

"Put to death, therefore whatever belongs to your earthly nature: sexual immorality, impurity, lust, evil desires and greed, which is idolatry. Because of these, the wrath of God is coming"—Colossians 3:5-6.

"But the cowardly, the unbelieving, the vile, the murderers, the sexually immoral, those who practice magic arts, the idolaters and all liars—their place will be in the fiery lake of burning sulfur. This is the second death''—Revelations 21:8.

Scriptures on being wholly committed to Christ:

"Therefore, I urge you, brothers, in view of God's mercy, to offer your bodies as living sacrifices, holy and pleasing to God—which is your spiritual worship. Do not conform any longer to the pattern of this world, but be transformed by the renewing of your mind. Then you will be able to test and approve what God's will is—his good, pleasing and perfect will''—Romans 12:1-2.

"But whatever was to my profit I now consider loss for the sake of Christ. What is more, I consider everything a loss compared to the surpassing greatness of knowing Christ Jesus my Lord, for whose sake I have lost all things. I consider them rubbish, that I may gain Christ and be found in him, not having a righteousness of my own that comes from the law, but that which is through faith in Christ—the righteousness that comes from God and is by faith. I want to know Christ and the power of his resurrection and the fellowship of sharing in his sufferings, becoming like him in his death, and so, somehow, to attain to the resurrection from the dead. Not that I have already obtained all this, or have already been made perfect, but I press on to take hold of that for which Christ Jesus took hold of me. Brothers, I do not consider myself yet to have taken hold of it. But one thing I do: Forgetting what is behind and straining toward what is ahead, I press on toward the goal to win the prize for which God has called me heavenward in Christ Jesus"—Philippians 3:7-14.

212

CONCLUSION

Several years ago I was in the Northeast holding a large crusade. Each night at the conclusion of the meeting, many people responded to the invitation to believe on the name of the Lord Jesus Christ and be saved.

After I left the stage the final night to go to a changing room with an associate, someone knocked on the door. I opened it to find a long line of people standing in the hallway wanting specific prayer.

It took over an hour to pray for everyone. The entire time I prayed for people, I noticed a young woman standing at the end of the line. Her turn finally came, and this is what she told me:

> Mr. Wilkerson, I attend a University located about five hours away by car. I came here with some of my friends to visit my mother for the weekend. We

heard about your meeting and decided to come tonight.

I came forward at the end of your message for prayer, but no one prayed with me. That's why I came to talk with you.

I'm nineteen years old. Eight years ago, my uncle, who was in his 40's at the time, began coming into my bedroom late at night. He wanted to have sex. I was only eleven! The first couple of times, I tried to fight him, but after that I just gave in and let him have his way. Somehow I believed that I had seduced him and that it was my fault.

This went on for two full years, and then he moved away. By that time it was too late for me. I've had sex since then with any guy who has wanted to, and I've been called every name in the book for "easy."

Besides all that, I've become hopelessly addicted to crack. I'm sure you can't help, Mr. Wilkerson, but I had to tell somebody.

That is when I stopped her. I said, "Jesus can change your life tonight, and you can be brand new."

Several of the ministers joined me in prayer, and we commanded every satanic spirit to take its hands off of this precious young woman. After some twenty minutes of prayer, she began to weep. Then she said two things I will never forget. She said,

> Jesus, forgive me for being angry at You. I thought all of this was Your fault, and I hated You for it. But tonight, Lord, I want You to forgive me.
>
> Also, Lord Jesus, please help my uncle to come to Christ! I forgive him for all of the terrible things he did to me. Please save him, Lord. He needs Jesus, too.

In that instant, freedom came to that girl's life. Not only did Christ forgive her, but she was able to forgive this wretched uncle for all the crimes he had committed against her.

As she turned to leave the office, she looked back at me and said, "Mr. Wilkerson, the only fear I have stems from the fact that I've developed such a terrible habit pattern in the area of sexual conduct. I'm afraid that when I get back to school in the morning I will fall right back in the old pattern again." So we all prayed that God would give her power to defeat Satan's attacks.

Several weeks later, I was going through some correspondence. As I shuffled through the many letters, I ran across a handwritten manuscript. It was from this young woman. Here was the story she related:

Mr. Wilkerson, I'm writing to tell you about the unbelievable victory that is happening in my life.

The night I walked out of the office where you and the other ministers prayed for me, I never dreamed I would face the devil's attack as soon as I did.

I met my girlfriends in the parking lot, and we got in the car for the five-hour ride back to the university. Sitting in the back seat, I laid my head back. I hoped to sleep the entire trip home.

We hadn't been driving for five minutes when all of a sudden I felt the car fill up with the presence of Satan. Having felt this many times before, I knew at that moment I was about to face my first great battle as a new Christian.

All of a sudden, I had a vision. It was so clear I felt like I was looking at a television set. The scene was a flashback to my old bedroom, and I was sitting on the bed as an eleven-year old. I saw my uncle open the door and walk in like he did the first time it ever happened.

My uncle reached out his arms and beckoned me to come to him. I had learned that those arms were very cruel. In that moment, sitting in that car,

I knew that if I yielded to my uncle's wishes I would go back to the university and remain the same.

The battle was on as we traveled at sixty miles per hour. The other girls in the car had no idea that the devil was trying to snuff out the work Jesus had done in my life that night.

As the vision continued, my uncle insisted that I come to him. Mr. Wilkerson, I was about to enter my uncle's arms as tears of pain poured down my cheeks. But then, hearing the door latch turn, I looked to see the door open a second time.

There, to my amazement, standing in the doorway with tears streaming down His face, was Jesus! He reached His nail-scarred hands in my direction and said, "Come unto me."

For the first time in my life, I realized that I had another door available to me. Turning away from my uncle's direction, I raced into the loving arms of my big brother Jesus.

Instantly, the vision was over, and I was weeping. My girlfriends asked me what was wrong. For the rest of the drive home I wept and repeated over and over again, "I'm free . . . I'm free . . . I'm free."

That was three weeks ago, and I want you to know that I'll never be the same again.

My friend, only Jesus can do that.

Relationship With God

This book has been about a very important part of your young adult years, namely your dating relationships. But there is something even more important—your relationship with the God who created you.

You can have a great dating life but still be empty. You can have clothes in fashion and lots of money but still be empty. You can have popularity, friends, a job, and a "together" family—but still be empty. The only thing that will fill that empty void is a relationship with Jesus Christ. You need to have peace with God.

God created the world to be a perfect place for mankind, but man rejected God's plan and chose a sinful way of life. Out of an overwhelming love, Jesus came to die on the cross to save us from our sin. The Bible says that the wages of sin is death. It also says, however, that the gift of God is eternal life through Jesus Christ. (See Romans 6:23.)

Just as man in the beginning had to choose God or sin, so do you. You see, the Bible also says that all have sinned. *All.* That means you and me. But although the wages of sin is death, Jesus came that we might have life and have it more abundantly. (See John 10:10.) The choice is yours.

Jesus loves you! Is there any reason you can't receive Him as your Savior and Lord right now?

Here's what you must do:

1. *Admit* your need ("I am a sinner").
2. Be willing to *turn* from your sins (repent).
3. *Believe* that the Lord Jesus Christ died for you on the cross and rose from the grave.
4. Through prayer, *invite* Jesus to come in and control your life (receive Him as Lord and Savior).

Please pray this prayer right now:

"Dear Lord Jesus,
I know I am a sinner, and I need your forgiveness. I believe that you died for my sins. I want to turn from my sins. Please come into my heart and life. I want to trust you as Savior and follow you as Lord, in the fellowship of Your Church. Amen."

I love you. God loves you—just as you are—and He sees all that you can become!

ABOUT THE AUTHOR

Pastor and evangelist, Rich Wilkerson focuses on the critical issues of our troubled society. An animated speaker and the author of several books, including *Carnal Christians and Other Words That Don't Go Together,* Rich delivers his powerful, candid message in churches and schools, at seminars, and on television.

For prayer, counseling, or comments, write to:

Rich Wilkerson
P.O. Box 1092
Tacoma, WA 98401

APPENDIX

SAMPLING OF SCRIPTURE PASSAGES
REFERRING TO SEX AND FAMILY
from
"Dating for Christians"
by Dr. Wayde Goodall

Genesis 1 & 2	Creation of male and female
Genesis 1:26-28	Sex relations in marriage
Genesis 26:8	Sex play before intercourse
Genesis 38:9	Avoiding conception
Genesis 38:9	Fornication
Exodus 22:16-17	Education
Exodus 22:19b	Bestiality
Leviticus 18:22, 23	Homosexuality
Leviticus 20:13	Incest
Leviticus 20:10	Adultery
Deuteronomy 22:23-27	Rape
Book of Hosea	Hosea's marriage to a harlot and his subsequent forgiveness is likened to the relationship between God and Israel as Israel plays the harlot and breaks her covenant with God

1 Samuel 2:22	Temple Prostitution
2 Samuel 11-22	David and Bathsheba (lust)
2 Samuel 13	Amnon and Tamar (lust)
Proverbs 5:18-20	Rejoice in your wife
Proverbs 23:27-28	Prostitution
Song of Solomon	Love poetry regarding Bride and Groom
Matthew 5:27-28	Adultery, Lust (Scripture silent on masturbation . . . this passage could relate)
Matthew 10:35-36	Family Relationship
Romans 1:19-27	Sex Deviations (e.g. homosexuality)
1 Corinthians 6:9-10, 15-25	Adultery
Matthew 15:9	Fornication
1 Corinthians 7:2-9	Marriage
1 Corinthians 7:5	Abstinence
1 Corinthians 7:10-11; Matthew 5:31-32; 19:3-19	Divorce
1 Corinthians 11:8-9	Woman created for man, submits freely and in joy to her husband
Galatians 5:19-21	Punishments for immorality
Ephesians 5:5	No immoral or impure man has any inheritance in the Kingdom of God
Ephesians 5:25	Love of husband and wife
Ephesians 5:28-33	Love of husband and wife
Colossians 3:18	Instructions to wives
1 Timothy 5:10, 14	Advice to mothers, widows
1 Peter 3	Instruction to wives and husbands
1 John 4:7-11	Love for one another

Marriage

Genesis 2:24
Matthew 19:5-6
John 2:1-22
1 Corinthians 7
Ephesians 5:22-23
1 Thessalonians 4:1-8

Family

Genesis 1:28; 2:24
Deuteronomy 6:1-15
Psalm 127:3-5; 128:3
Ephesians 5:22
Colossians 3:18-25

What The Bible Says About Sex

	Old Testament	New Testament
Sex	Sex is good in God's sight. Sex for pleasure is approved. Sex play is recognized as normal. Sex is openly discussed.	Sex is approved
Fornication	Forbidden	Forbidden
Adultery	Forbidden	Forbidden

	Old Testament	New Testament
Harlotry	Forbidden	Forbidden
Masturbation	Nothing stated	Nothing stated
Homosexuality	Forbidden	Forbidden
Bestiality	Forbidden, Condemned	
Incest	Forbidden	Forbidden
Rape	Forbidden	
Sex thoughts		Lustful thoughts should be controlled